Exotics and Erotics

Exotics and Erotics

Human Cultural and Sexual Diversity

DeWight R. Middleton

State University of New York College, Oswego

WAVELAND
PRESS, INC.
Long Grove, Illinois

For information about this book, contact:
Waveland Press, Inc.
4180 IL Route 83, Suite 101
Long Grove, IL 60047-9580
(847) 634-0081
info@waveland.com
www.waveland.com

Cover photo: Christina Hope/SuperStock

Contents

Preface

When I began teaching human sexuality a few years back, I could not find a text that would properly support my vision of the course. I discovered that the popular sexuality texts are large, unwieldy tomes that cover a wide variety of subtopics but are narrowly focused on contemporary American sexuality. I wanted something shorter and more flexible, with interdisciplinary input, and a wider temporal and cross-cultural perspective. I wrote this concise text with these criteria in mind, intending it to be used as either a basic or supplemental text. I learned quickly that the goal of writing a succinct text would force me to make many hard decisions about content and to bypass the many inviting side roads that mark the way. I hope that instructors will find this succinct treatment an instructional opportunity, rather than a drawback.

I wish to acknowledge my colleague, Paul Voninski, for providing me with a steady stream of current news about sexual matters. I want to thank Ivan Brady for his customary enthusiasm and support for this project, and for many years of discourse on pedagogical and intellectual matters. Our intellectual trails keep crossing each other in exciting ways. The anonymous reviewers made a number of critical and constructive comments that have improved the text immeasurably. I alone am responsible for any deficiencies it might have. It was a pleasure to work with Jeni Ogilvie and Tom Curtin at Waveland, and to benefit again from their friendly professionalism. As always, Peg, Leida, and Chandra inspired me.

Chapter One

A Panoramic View
of Sexuality

At the beginning of the twenty-first century, we face a challenging array of sexual issues ranging from old and continuing problems to new trends and future possibilities. Ancient problems of prostitution and rape persist but with new twists. Children in Nepal, India, and Thailand prostitute themselves for survival, while affluent high school girls in Japan do it for money in order to purchase trendy clothes at local malls. Rape now often occurs in the form of date rape, or as a result of women being drugged on social occasions, thus rendering them helpless to defend themselves against sexual assault. New trends include phone sex, cybersex, and an increasing sexual content in television programming around the world. In North America, television movie channels now show "soft porn" during late night hours, and sexual humor and situations saturate evening sitcoms. The AIDS epidemic continues, but receives so much attention that it masks the fact that the United States has the highest incidence of sexually transmitted diseases (STDs) in the industrial world. Advocates of sexual freedom war with sexual conservatives. Homosexuality, present in human sexual behavior from the beginning, still stirs heated controversy. New sexual technologies, for example, customized virtual sex, raise questions about the future of intimate relationships. Viagra, the pill that aids penile erection in legitimate cases of sexual dysfunction, is used by those with no such problem, raising questions of abuse. Can an orgasm pill for women be far behind?

It is a paradox that in a time when we are awash in information about sex we know much less about it than we think we do. Being

1

poorly informed leaves us adrift in today's churning sexual sea with no sure compass to direct us through its many conflicting currents. How are we to solve problems, legislate effectively, and teach wisely about sex without a clear perspective and solid information? Certainly there are scores of experts and gurus available to tell us about our sexuality, and while they are often helpful, they are also narrowly focused on sexual techniques, physiology, and North American sexuality. We view them regularly on television talk shows or can easily find their popular books at local bookstores. We can view myriad sexual messages of varying degrees of explicitness and accuracy on television and hear them in popular music; they are created by people who know little more about sex than the ordinary person. Because they come from different sources with different intentions, these messages are necessarily mixed and contradictory. Sexual activism, sex education, and sexual violence all compete for our attention but are more likely to provoke emotional outbursts than informed discussion.

How well prepared is the average person to work his/her way through this buzzing confusion? A Time/CNN (1998) poll of American teenagers indicated that 45 percent of them obtained their information about sex from each other, and 29 percent got it from television. Only 3 percent said that they acquired their information from sex education, while 7 percent indicated their parents as their source. Whether or not these figures are precisely accurate, and the true picture is certainly more complex than a questionnaire can reveal, they are generally consistent with what scholars and workers in the field know—that our knowledge of one of the most powerful forces in human life is limited, fragmented, and generally deficient.

These limitations impair our ability to think effectively about sexuality issues. Specifically, our understanding fails to measure up in five important ways:

1. We acquire *piecemeal* what we know of human sexuality.

2. We fix narrowly on our *local* sexual experience, which limits a wider vision.

3. We focus on sexual issues that are *current*.

4. We treat sexuality as an *isolated* phenomenon.

5. We too often confuse *labels* with reality.

Where knowledge of sexuality is normally acquired in bits and pieces, this text provides a comprehensive framework by which to organize facts and interpret sexual diversity in all times and places. Because this framework is based on cross-cultural and historical studies, it counters the limiting influence of our local and contemporary cultural experience by describing the range of sexualities that defines the human sexual condition in different places and times. This panoramic view will balance our tendency to focus narrowly on current problems and encourage us see them in the cross-cultural range of other problems and possibilities. Human sexuality in general, and local sexualities specifically, cannot be understood properly when isolated from their historical and cultural contexts. In fact, sexuality is shaped by many social forces often unrecognized by the participants themselves. Human sexuality then must be understood to be firmly imbedded in wider cultural meanings and social relationships. Discussions of human sexuality normally rely on unreliable concepts and labels. We tend to treat labels as real, rather than as representations of reality, and therefore are not sufficiently critical of their accuracy. Unexamined labels can distort reality and often provoke emotional responses that hinder enlightened discourse. This text aims to remedy these deficiencies and constructs a well-marked chart to travel a sure course through the rapidly shifting currents of modern sexuality.

Although it is fundamentally anthropological in its approach, this exploration of sexuality draws on other disciplines, because human sexuality is complex and in the end engages the efforts of many academic disciplines and theoretical perspectives. The term *sexuality* in fact connotes the *wider social, cultural, and psychological environments in which sexual desires are enacted*. The text however, does not address sexual hygiene and therapy, the biology of human reproduction, or having good sexual relationships, as is so often the case with standard college textbooks. These texts are certainly valuable but are devoted to different tasks. Nor does this text assert a particular sexual morality. It instead describes and analyzes sexualities in different times and places. It does not claim that we know everything we need to know about human sexuality, nor does it assert that we can fully understand every sexuality that we encounter, but it does advance the idea that we know enough to make good sense of most human sexual behavior.

Although the title, *Exotics and Erotics*, might be considered provocative to some, I chose it after careful thought about how best to characterize the theme of the text, which is understanding human and sexual diversity. If it is also provocative, it is so for good reason. These words, or labels, if you will, in our culture and language are heavily invested with emotional and sexual meaning. As written words they catch the eye, much as sex does. Erotic, of course, refers to sexual desire and arousal. What is erotic is what we find sexually stimulating. A state of arousal combines cultural, psychological, and biological elements of our existence, hence the complexity of human sexuality. The biological elements may be constant among all human *groups*, but cultures vary in what they find to be erotic. Female breasts as an example are not a focus of erotic interest in all cultures. Eroticism does not exist in a cultural vacuum, but is immersed in concepts of beauty, gender, and even political and economic arrangements.

Exotic refers to the strange, alien, and different. There are two important connotations to the word, exotic, that link it with erotic. First, we are imaginative and creative beings as well as creatures of custom and routine. We can imagine variety and fantasize about people and situations that feed eroticism—sex is in the brain we are told—otherwise we would routinely perform plain acts of reproduction, vanilla sex, without the spices. As a playful and creative species, we can experiment sexually to produce new varieties and nuances of sexual feeling. This is a form of exoticism that exists within our own culture, our own psyche.

There is a second meaning to exotic that culturally combines the exotic and the erotic. Anthropologists are sometimes accused of being intellectual curiosity seekers, endlessly searching for the exotic culture, for what is new and different. Regardless of the truth of this charge, and there is some, anthropologists are not alone in this desire to discover new and strange (exotic) lives. But curiosity about others is not a purely intellectual matter as the history of Western travel and discovery shows us. There is an erotic side to human thoughts about other peoples. Novelty can feed (or repel) our sexual imagination and thus can be powerfully erotic to us. Westerners, for example, often find the physical appearance of peoples of the South Pacific to be attractive. We imagine them leading a highly erotic life on a verdant, tropical island in a boundless blue sea. Travel advertisements for the South Pacific play heavily on this seductive image.

THE SEXUAL OTHER

The image of an idyllic, tropical life of sexual freedom and graceful living associated with the alluring Polynesians has long held an irresistible appeal to disgruntled Westerners. The French painter, Paul Gauguin, is a famous example of a Westerner who, no longer at ease with his life in Europe, acted to make his dream of living the sensuous life come true. The appeal of the south seas to Gauguin, however, was more complex than simple sexuality. Plagued by family and money worries, he left a destitute and marginal life as an artist in Europe for the easy sensuality of life in the Pacific. He eagerly anticipated the day of departure.

> May the day come (soon perhaps) when I can go off and escape to the woods of some South Seas island and live there in ecstasy, in peace, and in art. With a new family, far from this European struggle for money. There, in Tahiti, in the still of beautiful tropical nights, I shall be able to listen to the soft, murmuring music of my heart beating in loving harmony with the mysterious creatures

around me. Free at last, with no money worries, I shall love, sing, and die. (quoted in Le Pichon 1987:113)

Gauguin's departure from Europe was both an *escape* from the cold reality of his circumstances there and a *search* for a warmer poetic life, one more sympathetic in his mind to his artistic sensibilities. He was searching for the exotic trigger to his artistic imagination and for a peaceful release from care and debt. The themes of mystery, harmony, love, and sensuality are all present in this brief quotation. They are common Western projections onto the lives of the peoples of the South Pacific.

Gauguin was not much interested in forming a clear understanding of the people with whom he lived, but merely in painting them and their colorful environment while escaping from responsibilities at home. He arrived in Tahiti on June 8, 1891, at the age of 43, and he was soon confronted with the reality that Tahiti was not the untouched paradise that he imagined it to be. Attending the funeral of King Pomare V, who died almost immediately after his arrival, Gauguin comments: "When he died so did Maori tradition. Now it was really done for. Alas, civilization with its soldiery, trade, and officialdom triumphed" (quoted in Le Pichon 1987:147). Nevertheless, he soon settled into a rustic life and, after a series of native mistresses, married a thirteen-year-old girl in a traditional Tahitian marriage ceremony. With this union he seemed more than ever seduced by the sensuality and fragrance of oiled bodies and the scents of tropical flowers—a visual feast for an artist—all in a south seas paradise of endless white beaches bordered by graceful palm trees. This was the life he had dreamed of, but the dream remained illusionary, for even in Tahiti he found that he needed money. He had no way of earning it because there was no market for his paintings on the island. They had to be sent to Europe by sea and did not sell quickly. There were few other opportunities for work, and he could not even hold those modest jobs that he did attempt. His meager funds depleted after only two years in Tahiti, and he was forced to return to Europe.

His dream remained alive, however, and he returned to Tahiti in 1895 and married another native girl of fourteen and a half. But again his dream was not to be fully realized. Sick with a variety of illnesses, he moved on to the Marquesas in 1901 where he took still another native wife, but died two years later, in debt, in his home, which he had named the "House of Pleasure." In Gauguin's view of the Polynesians and their sensual island life, sexual and cultural diversity are thus intermingled and the exotic and the erotic joined.

Paradoxically, erotic images of others ultimately may say as much about us as they do about exotic natives. The different sexual practices and attitudes of other people can be used against them as well as for them, either way reducing them to unidimensional caricatures of themselves and robbing them of their full humanity. Describing Polynesians in terms of their traditional sexuality falls far short of defining who they are as complete human beings. Throughout history, Westerners have tended to cast onto "primitive" cultures their own sexual and cultural concerns; that is, native peoples are intellectually and emotionally used by Westerners to comment (that is, to criticize or support) on troubling aspects of their own culture.

"Savages" have been characterized as either noble and a symbol of the innocence civilization has lost or as truly savage and a reminder of how far civilization has progressed. Sexuality is an issue in both cases. In the former case, Westerners can imagine the simple sexuality of "innocence" not yet lost by native peoples (as did Gauguin), while in the latter they can be contemptuous of animalistic and lustful sexuality not yet controlled. The two views reflect divisions in our own culture regarding sexuality. Of course, our view of native peoples is not necessarily their reality. Unfortunately, our images of them are not just idle mind play but bear real consequences for them historically because of our ability to exert power over their lives. Generally, the historical Western and Christian view is that savagery requires pacification and unbridled sexuality requires cultural and religious controls. As a result of these beliefs, our actions toward them usually have been based more on our cultural biases than on our understanding their behaviors and therefore are destructive of their culture and identity.

It is important to understand that *all* human groups—not just Westerners—use others in similar ways. The Polynesians did not understand us at first any better than we understood them and felt superior to us in some ways. All of us are to a degree *ethnocentric*—centered in our own culture. Stereotypes of others, whether or not they are sexually based, are constructed to satisfy their makers; to say that the enemy are monsters justifies killing them, that others are savages makes us feel better about ourselves, and that still others are equal encourages us to share with them. These "others" do not have to occupy distant, exotic islands. They live among us. A person with different sexual interests can be the "other." Different racial or ethnic groups can be the "other." All human groups live today in a culturally complex and diverse world. Human diversity in whatever form is a condition of human life that requires our informed attention and our discovery of the real people behind stereotypes.

Although not reflected in the title, this text underscores the importance of recognizing the ongoing problem of individuals fitting into specific cultural contexts with particular reference to sexuality. While it is true that our own culture shapes our sexuality in general, we are not clones and do not lose entirely our individuality. Probably all humans have some personal sexual desires and fantasies that would not be considered mainstream in their culture. So each individual is at least a bit different sexually. While we will focus on the social and cultural aspects of sexuality, some consideration will be given to this individual level of sexuality as well, for it is an integral part of the comprehensive framework required to complete our task here. Individual sexuality, mainstream or not, is intimately tied up with roles, genders, identities, and ideas of self that help define both the social and sexual person.

TO THE STUDENT

The anthropological perspective is one that combines universal human sexuality with its local manifestations in specific cultural contexts; it also explores how the individual is integrated into a culture. References to the individual in a cultural context should aid you in taking more from this text than is written. By considering your own reactions to what you read here, you will develop some personal understanding about how your sexuality is shaped by the culture and times in which you live, by the people with whom you interact, and by your own particular experiences in life even if they do not appear to you to be unique. Where, for example, do your ideas and values regarding sexuality come from? How do you fit with the Time/CNN poll cited earlier? Do you think you are very different, or are you basically mainstream? Where do you stand on issues and why?

Students come to class with many different sexual experiences, attitudes, and values. As suggested above, some of what you read in this text will challenge those beliefs and experiences. With respect to sexual morality, for example, consider whether your judgments about the sexual values and behaviors of others, even in your own culture, are based more on cultural or religious beliefs, on science, or on your own unique viewpoint. In spite of what has been described as a sea of sexual messages that washes over us daily, there are still many individuals who are sensitive about their sexuality and about sexuality in general. Those who feel this way may be startled by some of the frank references to sexual acts and sexual anatomy contained in this text. Various sexual issues discussed herein may arouse your emotions and lead you to spirited exchanges of opinions with others. These reactions are a necessary part of the learning process and, in fact, tell you more about your own values and beliefs than you might have known before; on the other hand, they might further confirm your present take on sexuality. Encountering these sexualities might give you a mild case of *culture shock,* a condition that people often experience in heavier doses when visiting another culture. The frustrations of dealing with another way of life that you don't understand very well can be irritating and even debilitating. Anthropologists in the field use such shocks, challenges, and confrontations to learn more about others *and* themselves. I hope that you accept the challenge.

PORNOGRAPHIC POTS AND CLASSICAL SEX

Graphic representations of sexual anatomy and acts appear early in our ancient past, although their meaning is unclear. In 1908, a small figure (about five inches tall) of a female with large breasts and buttocks, and bearing traces of red ochre, was discovered near the Danube River in Austria. This figurine dates back to the last Ice Age (12,000 to 40,000 years ago) (Taylor 1997:116). It was found at an archaeological site called Willendorf II, and the figure is known as the Venus of Willendorf. Actually, it is one of a couple of hundred such suggestive female figurines unearthed in the twentieth century, and dating to the Ice Age. The meaning that these "Venuses" conveyed to their viewers is not known, but rather is a matter of speculation as Taylor observes. Are they Ice Age pornography, goddesses of fertility, mother goddesses, instruments of sorcery, or portraits of real people (Taylor 1997:116)? The figurines are not uniform in their appearance. They were made at different times and places, emphasizing different parts of the body. They probably conveyed at least slightly different meanings, some of which perhaps had to do with sexuality and fertility. We see these ancient images from our contemporary point of view and therefore risk projecting our current perspectives onto these figures without any well-defined cultural contexts or written records to guide us. Some of these figurines, for example, might be more about fertility and group continuity at a time when mortality rates were high and life expectancy quite low than about erotic sex divorced from reproduction, an image that increasingly reflects the perspective of Western cultures. Even anthropological textbooks are inconsistent and incomplete in their treatment of these figures (Nelson 2001).

We know even less about the phallic batons of the Paleolithic than we do the Venuses. These batons are clearly depictions of penises, including a double headed penis. Are they symbols of fertility, power? Ritual objects? Dildos? We can only guess. Like the Venuses, they are explicit renderings of sexual anatomy and among the very first artistic efforts of humans. The Grave of the Golden Penis (Taylor 1997:175–77) was discovered on the Black Sea coast of present-day Bulgaria, and dates to about 4,000 B.C. The skeleton of a man was laid out in the grave, on his back, with the golden penis placed in the anatomically appropriate position. Again the question, what does it mean? There is no definitive answer.

Many past cultures have fashioned explicit images of sexual behavior. The Mochica of coastal Peru made sexually explicit pottery prior to 1000 A.D. The pottery commonly depicted heterosexual intercourse, fellatio, cunnilingus, male masturbation, and bestiality of various kinds. About a third of the images were of heterosexual anal intercourse, and 3 percent were of homosexual anal intercourse. A quarter of them showed the penis, usually erect, but only 4 percent showed the vulva (Bullough 1976:41–42). There is no explanation as to why there were so many images of heterosexual anal intercourse. Although the potters were women, the more frequent renderings of the penis possibly reflect a male-centered culture. There is, again, no way to be sure. These prehistoric images further testify to the long history of our need to depict graphically, for whatever reasons, various forms of sexual activity.

The historical record continues this line of explicit sexual images with written references to sexual activity and attitudes. The early cultures of Mesopotamia, Persia, Sumer, and Babylon worshipped fertility as a life force. Life force is more than simple sexuality; it includes uneasiness about group and family continuity in the context of a normally short life span due to disease and violence. In this context, women were especially valued for their ability to procreate. They were also considered to be property, and thus adultery was a violation of a man's property rights and not a sin. The Sumerians, who established Mesopotamia around 3000 B.C., were literate. The Sumerian symbol for fertility was the sexual act, and the symbols for males and females were depictions of sexual parts. The Sumerians were sexually accepting, homosexuality was tolerated, and anal intercourse was apparently frequent.

Ancient Greeks were known to be tolerant of homosexuality, particularly among men. But as their first obligation, all men had to marry and produce children. Women's activities were restricted, and their principal role was to procreate. Greek culture was a "sex positive" culture (Bullough 1976), with an appreciation of sensory experiences, and an admiration of nudity in specific situations, for example, in sports. Statues of phalluses were common in public places and were used in certain religious ceremonies. The Greeks also created explicit pictures of sexual activity, including homosexuality, on vases known as amphorae. Greek men were warriors as well as intellectuals, and they idealized male strength and beauty. They formed military clubs, for example, that fostered male relationships and homosexuality.

Homosexuality was not evenly spread across the various Greek city-states and social classes; it was mostly an upper-class activity and was not considered proper between same-age males. Instead, it was restricted to relationships between older men and youths in their middle and late teens and was based on an adherence to the values and ideals of a male-centered society. Homosexuality in this case was not supposed to be the object of the relationship, but often turned out to be so. It was considered to be a passing phase of life, and a heterosexual life was expected to follow it. The ideal was not necessarily followed by everyone, but those who did not conform to norms risked ridicule and a damaged reputation. While lesbian relationships were probably formed, especially because of limited female association with males, little is known about them because they were not as public as male homosexuality. Sappho was an acclaimed poet who wrote about love and friendship among women and spent most of her time in the company of other women on the Island of Lesbos—hence the term Lesbian—where she ran a school for girls, but little is known of the details of her life. To what degree she actually participated in lesbian sexual affairs is unknown.

In Rome, women were considered the property of men, but their status still was somewhat higher than among Greeks. Although public nudity and homosexuality were not appreciated, Romans in fact tolerated a range of sexual practices and prostitution. Entertainment preceding the gladiatorial contests included public sexual activities. After the contests, male patrons could go with prostitutes to places under public buildings, arches known as *cellae fornicae*, from which derived the word *fornication*. Indeed, many sexual terms such as *fellatio, cunnilingus*, and *masturbation* are Latin terms. As Vern Bullough (1976:129–30) notes, the word *phallus* was borrowed from the Greek to refer to the penis. But the Latin term, *fascinum* (the origin of the English, fascinate), is the proper term, because it more accurately communicates the potent power of the penis and public fascination with the phallus. Because of their power, phallic statues were placed at city gates and outside shops as protection against enemies and misfortune. Children wore phallic amulets around their necks to guard against the evil eye. The female pudenda was regarded as a symbol of generative power and usually represented by a shell, but had less public presence than the phallus. Other sexual images were present in ancient Rome, such as brothel coins that portrayed the sexual act to be purchased. Middle- and upper-class residences in Pompeii frequently featured sexually explicit murals in their living rooms.

Ancient Hebrew sexual practices had perhaps the most lasting and profound influence on Western sexuality. The Hebrews believed that sexual intercourse was for procreation only. Sexual relations outside of marriage were unacceptable. In cases of adultery, the woman faced punishment by death, but a man, while possibly punished severely, escaped death. A woman was considered to be the property of a husband or a father. Indeed, a father could sell a daughter's sexual services. These ideas were influential in early Christianity, which Bullough classifies as a sex-negative religion (although he also cautions that it was not at that time a unified religion). In fact, Christianity was influenced not only by Hebrew culture, but also by some countercurrents in Greek philosophy. Competing philosophies raised issues about the value of the soul over the sensory experiences of the body. These philosophical schools were known as epicureans, stoics, and cynics (Bullough 1976:159–60).

The historical record clearly shows that we displayed very early in our history a keen and explicit interest in sexuality. It is clear, too, from this brief historical account that different cultures handle sexual desires and activities in different ways. Bullough (1976) uses the general classification of sex-positive and sex negative-cultures to characterize the dominant attitudes toward sex in various historical societies. Yet, this general classification eventually leads to further questions about why this should be so and how cultural guidance toward positive and negative sexual viewpoints actually work in practice. These are convenient general categories that, however, are frozen in time and oversimplify a more complex reality, therefore having quite limited use today.

STUDYING HUMAN SEXUALITY

Some of the earliest writings on sexuality were devoted to increasing sexual pleasure. Among the oldest and most famous are, *The Kama Sutra*, or "Precepts of Pleasure," from Ancient India and *The Perfumed Garden*, translated from the Arabic in the eighteenth century. In Europe, in 1524, Gulio Romano rendered drawings of sixteen coital positions from which he then made engravings for wider distribution, leading to a scandal; the authorities considered them obscene. Their reaction led to the creation of the *Index of Prohibited Books*, in 1559, an early attempt at censorship. Meanwhile, science and medicine turned to studies of reproduction and sexually transmitted diseases. Antonie van Leeuwenhoek (1632–1723), for example, first observed spermatozoa in semen through his microscope in 1677, and medical concerns arose over the spread of syphilis and gonorrhea following European voyages of exploration in the 1500s. This early attention to sexually transmitted diseases proved an important impetus to the scientific study of sexuality. In the closing decades of the eighteenth century more scholars became interested in studying the subject. In 1758, Simon Andre Tissot (1728–1797) published *Onanism: Dissertation on the Sickness Produced by Masturbation*, in which he alleged that masturbation produced insanity if not idiocy, thus negatively influencing Western attitudes toward autoeroticism to this day.

Iwan Bloch (1872–1922) is generally considered to be the founder of sexology (he coined the term) along with Richard von Krafft-Ebing (1840–1902), a neurologist and psychiatrist, who published *Sexual Pa-*

thologies in 1886. Bloch, a physician, confined his studies to historical and anthropological documents (Gregersen 1996:28). Krafft-Ebing compiled a list of variations in sexual practice based on his accumulation of some 200 case studies. In 1908, Magnus Hirschfeld (1868–1935) founded the *Journal of Sexual Science*, and the Medical Society for Sexology and Eugenics. The rise of the eugenics movement, defined as selective breeding for the good of humanity, is important because it signaled the joining of scientific forces with social movements advocating birth control and greater sexual freedom. By 1904, Hirschfeld had collected over 10,000 sexual histories. He claimed that based on these histories there were over two million homosexuals in Germany. This idea was not popular with the Nazis who thought that they were members of a superrace, therefore without such weaknesses, and consequently they burned the histories in 1933.

Havelock Ellis (1868–1935) published a series of studies on the psychological aspects of sex that later were condensed into a single volume summary, the *Psychology of Sex* (1933). He argued that homosexuality is not a matter of choice and that insanity is not linked to masturbation. Sigmund Freud (1856–1939) devoted his life to psychoanalysis, much of which was premised on the human sex drive in the form of the *libido* and its influence on individual development through the life cycle. He saw the individual's natural drive toward self-gratification being continually frustrated by the constraints of culture and thus producing psychological problems and compensations. He also speculated about sexuality in other cultures. In *Totem and Taboo* (1913) he claimed (based on his clinical studies in Europe) that the Oedipus complex, the son's conflict with his father over the affections of his mother, is universal. With this assertion he ventured into anthropological territory, inviting criticism by anthropologists of his claim of the universality of the Oedipus complex. Alfred Kinsey (1894–1956), a zoologist, led the Institute for Sexual Research, which was formed at Indiana University in 1947. Based on extensive interviewing, the Kinsey Institute published the first major work on sexuality in the United States, *Sexual Behavior of the Human Male*, in 1948, followed by one on female sexuality in 1953. Masters and Johnson (1966, 1970, 1979) made extensive physiological investigations into human sexual performance and operated a clinic in St. Louis for those with sexual dysfunction.

In anthropology, Bronislaw Malinowski (1884–1942) did the premier work on sexuality with his study of the Trobriand Islands, which lie just off the southern tip of New Guinea in the South Pacific, not far from northern Australia. Malinowski spent two years there during World War I and earned his fame largely through his exhaustive description and thorough analysis of the Trobrianders in a number of articles and books published in the 1920s and 1930s. In his *The Sexual Life of Savages* (1987; orig. 1929) he describes Trobriand sexual practices and attitudes in the full context of their culture. The Trobriand case shows that human sexuality is never a simple matter of biological coupling, but as Malinowski noted is a potent "sociological and cultural force" (p. xxxiii). Malinowski therefore argued for the full contextualization of studies of sexuality (or any other cultural practice for that matter) in order to make sense of how human sexuality is shaped by culture and how it is related to other practices and institutions. As a part of his approach, he advocated seeing sexuality from the natives' point of view. That is, we need to develop a model of their lifeway that reflects as closely as possible their way of organizing and interpreting their reality. With his study of Trobriand sexuality, Malinowski set early standards for the proper field study of human sexual practice, most of which are still valid for the twenty-first century.

In a famous dispute that underscores the importance of context, Malinowski disagreed with Freud's idea of a universal Oedipus complex. He argued to the contrary that conflict and tension between son and father had more to do with nonsexual emotions such as the son's resistance to his father's power and authority in a patriarchal, *patrilineal* (descent traced through the male line) European culture. In contrast, he discovered with the Trobrianders, who had a *matrilineal* system with family authority vested in the mother's oldest brother, that relations between son and father were cordial and relaxed, while tension suffused the relationship between the mother's son and his uncle—the mother's brother. Thus he found Freud's focus on sexuality as a source of conflict to be too restrictive. Malinowski's rejection of the universality of the Oedipus complex effectively shifted sexuality from the psychological to the cultural level of investigation as a prerequisite to psychological study (Weiner 1987:xxxi). This shift was consistent with the popularity at the time of such topics as the evolution of family systems, primitive mentality, and sexuality, and thus Malinowski's contribution was well received.

To proponents of the scientific study of sexuality, such as Havelock Ellis, the early sexologist who wrote the preface and predicted it would be a classic, Malinowski's study was a most welcome contribution to the developing scientific literature on sexuality (see Weiner 1987). There are several important points to be made regarding Malinowski's famous study. (1) The publication of this account coincided with the increasing legitimacy of the scientific study of human sexuality in the West, but with English and American public reticence to encounter sexuality still the norm. (2) It resonated with Western fascination with exotic and erotic practices of so-called primitive people, in contrast to "civilized" and Christian sexuality. (3) It presented sexual practices and values in a cultural context, showing how Trobriand sexuality was related to other aspects of culture. (4) While the apparent sexual freedom it described made an indelible impression on the reader because of its novelty at the time and its consistency with some Western stereotypes of primitive culture, many readers no doubt remembered less well Malinowski's lengthy description of Trobriand cultural control over, and moral constraints on, their sexual behavior. Counter to stereotype, traditional Trobrianders did not engage in unfettered sexuality.

Margaret Mead (1901–1978) conducted three early studies into sex role behavior and adolescent development: *Coming of Age in Samoa* (1928), *Growing Up in New Guinea* (1930), and *Sex and Temperament in Three Primitive Societies* (1950; orig. 1935). Although there are discussions of young female love affairs in the Samoa ethnography, now controversial, she wrote mainly about human development and sex role behavior rather than providing the more detailed descriptions of sexuality as reported by Malinowski. In the 1950s, Clelland S. Ford and Frank A. Beach published *Patterns of Sexual Behavior* (1951). Nearly 200 societies were included in this cross-cultural survey of various aspects of human sexuality. Although the reported coverage on sexuality was uneven across the sample of ethnographies, the survey supplied a good and timely overview of human sexuality based on reasonably solid reporting. Michel Foucault's (1926–1984) three-volume work, *The History of Sexuality* (1978, 1985, 1986), has been enormously influential, although often criticized among Western social scientists and social historians. Writing about power, self, and sex, he focuses on how our subjectivity and sexuality are shaped by forces outside of our individual selves. He argues, for example, that twentieth-century medicine exerted a form of control, a "medicalization," over our sex lives by diagnosing normal and abnormal sex and prescribing treatment for acts such as masturbation. Foucault, like Malinowski earlier, also contributed to a shift in attention from a "psychologised" repressed sexuality about which Freud theorized to sexuality at the sociocultural level.

METHODS OF STUDY

Modern methods of studying human sexuality include most of those used routinely by the social sciences and psychology as well as historical documentation. A brief survey of these methods will provide the necessary basis upon which we can critically appraise their validity and accuracy. We cannot entertain here an extended treatment of methods, but we can develop a sufficient awareness of the advantages and disadvantages of the principal approaches by means of a brief overview.

Participant observation. Anthropologists rely heavily on participant observation to enable them to uncover the full substance of cultural life. This hybrid term accurately labels an inherent tension in fieldwork. On the one hand, anthropologists are outsiders wishing to *observe* the insiders, the members of the culture under study. On the other hand, they are outsiders who wish to *participate* in the activities and organizations of the insiders in order to experience the culture as an insider. Ideally, anthropologists try to strike a balance between participation and observation. But this is easier said than done and depends on local contingencies and the personality of the anthropologist. The tension lies in the fear that being too much of an observer might remove the anthropologist too far from the insider experience, while going to the extreme of participation positions the anthropologist too close to the insiders, thereby losing objectivity. For example, observing the spring planting is different from actually engaging in planting so that you truly understand the skill and effort it requires. Participating in an event might prompt the observer to ask new questions that lead to deeper insight. But should an anthropologist take hallucinogenic drugs in order to probe the inner mysteries of a religion (Harner 1968)? Striking the balance is the art of doing fieldwork.

Participant observation is inefficient in the short run but pays off in the long run because it aids in building rapport with *informants* (those willing to teach outsiders about their culture), allows time for cross-checking information, and permits observations of actual behavior compared with stated norms. In general, it has yielded richly detailed studies of other cultures. Although many facets of sexuality are open to easy observation in most cultures, recording explicit sex usually will be a sensitive matter, and beyond the possibility of direct observation. Some anthropologists, however, are now coming forward to reveal the extent of their own sexual participation in other cultures (Kulick and Willson 1995).

Questionnaires and surveys. We are all accustomed to survey questionnaires. We see the results of them every day in public opinion polls done by telephone as in the Time/CNN poll discussed earlier. They can be very effective as indicated by how early in the evening newscasters "call" winners in state and national elections. Over the decades national pollsters have refined their understanding of the social characteristics of voters so that only very small samples (or portions) of the total population need be surveyed to deliver reliable data. Usually, the survey *respondents* (contrast this word with *informants* as in participant-observation) answer a structured set of questions that presumably make some sense to the respondent and allows him or her to make a relevant reply. The questions must be relevant to the issue at hand, they must be phrased properly so as to elicit the appropriate data, and they must make sense to those who respond to them. In some surveys, the questions might be "open ended" so that the respondent can expand on the question as he or she wishes. Ideally, the questionnaire should have internal checks (for example, the same question is asked in different ways to check for consistency of the answers).

Competently addressing these critical points assumes that those who construct the questionnaire know well the population to be tested.

As mentioned earlier, surveys are not usually given to each individual or unit in a population. A *population* is the defined group to be tested, and to which any conclusion from the survey applies. Because it is often impossible, inconvenient, or costly to reach every member of a population, researchers survey only *sample* portions of the population. For example, when Kinsey et al. surveyed sexual behavior in males and females, they started with a sample of convenience—whoever they could get to talk to them. Which happened to be college students, faculty, and prison inmates. Their first results then applied more to interested college faculty and students then it did to the entire population. *Playboy* magazine once did a mail survey of its readers, one-third of whom said that they had participated in group sex. Is this finding representative of the sexual behavior of non-*Playboy* readers? It is not because it is a self-selected group.

Survey results can establish correlations of a positive or negative kind. For example, the finding that there is a positive correlation between a college education and oral sex means that college-educated people are more likely to engage in oral sex than noncollege-educated people. A negative correlation would mean that there is no relationship at all between higher education and oral sex. The positive correlation does not mean that all college graduates engage in oral sex or that those who are not do not. The relationship between a higher level of education and oral sex is a correlation, but what is the cause? Does more education directly cause oral sex, indirectly cause it, or is there still another cause behind both of them?

Clinical studies. Freud's explorations of childhood sexuality in the course of treating his patients were based on his clinical cases. Such studies focus on individuals, or specific events, and can yield richly detailed, in-depth, results. Clinical studies can yield insights into cause, motivation and psychological dynamics that might be difficult for surveys to uncover. When Masters and Johnson studied sexual function and performance in St. Louis in the 1960s, they did not directly observe sexual performance but used innovative techniques, such as an artificial penis with a light in it, to measure sexual response. These studies yielded valuable information that led to improvements in sex therapy.

THE ANTHROPOLOGICAL APPROACH

Anthropology is the study of humans in all times and places, and in all aspects. This admittedly ambitious undertaking has stimulated the creation of many specialities that examine particular aspects of human life. These various specialities can be organized into four major subdivisions of the discipline. *Archaeology* is a subdivision of anthropology that studies the remains of past cultures and settlements such as Mayan temples and Mochican pottery in an effort to reconstruct the lifeways of those who created them. Physical or *biological anthropology* focuses on human evolution, human reproductive strategies, biological adaptability and diversity, genetics, primate behavior, and disease and medicine. *Anthropological linguistics* studies linguistic structures and behavior, social performance—*sociolinguistics*—and language acquisition in human development. The majority of anthropologists, however, are *cultural anthropologists*, (or sociocultural anthropologists) studying the social and cultural aspects of living people. This text draws principally on cultural anthropology, although it will include insights from other subdivisions as necessary.

Cultural anthropology discovers, describes, and seeks to explain human social and cultural lives. The notion of discovery in anthropology is quite important because fieldworkers such as Malinowski and Mead, in the early twentieth century, were discovering new cultures (although those cultures had already been contacted if not adequately described). The idea of discovery remains important today because it emphasizes the need to continue to approach even supposedly well-known cultures and subcultures with the fresh attitude that much remains to be known. For example, Annette Weiner (1976) published her own productive reexamination of aspects of Trobriand culture from a female point of view decades after Malinowski's exhaustive studies. Accurate *description* of cultural ways maintains the data quality control so important to good science. But this description must be based on direct experience in the culture being described, not always an easy task in reality. *Explanation* attempts to answer the how and why questions that lead to better understanding. In this text, we ask how is sexuality formed and why does it take the patterns it does in different cultures? Explanation is often not a simple matter because it gets entangled with competing theoretical perspectives, as revealed in the conflict between Malinowski and Freud over the Oedipus complex.

Anthropology's strategy toward achieving these goals features three central ideas. First, is the requirement that the *ethnographer* (the person doing the study) must live and work in the society he or she describes. The numerous and detailed ethnographies that make up the database for anthropological theorizing and understanding today were almost all done in the twentieth century by trained anthropologists who lived with the people about whom they reported. The goals of fieldwork are to live in the community of study for a year or two at least, learn the language if possible, and get to know the culture as deeply as conditions permit. Anthropologists have been achieving these goals for well over 100 years. In the end, the basic test of success is whether or not the fieldworker can function as a fully competent adult in that culture.

Cultural anthropology relies quite heavily on the large number of ethnographies that have been published over the past century; they constitute its essential database. Yet, these ethnographies were not only published at different times, but they represent cultures that are in various stages of change. Note the references earlier to the *traditional* Polynesians, and the *traditional* Trobrianders. The Polynesians and Trobrianders of ethnographic fame no longer exist as they were. (Remember Gauguin's lament that the Polynesians were already changing.) How much they have changed, and in what ways is another discovery to be made. The fact is, they often have been characterized as they existed in the nineteenth century (the Polynesians) and early in the twentieth century (the Trobrianders) at the times they were encountered and described. This is called the *ethnographic present*, and we should be alert to its misuse for it has the unintended effect of freezing people in time as if they always have been and always will be as recorded by the ethnographer. No culture is forever unchanging.

The second strategy of cultural anthropology is to compare richly detailed studies of different cultures with each other in an effort to discern cross-cultural patterns and variations. This *comparative* approach helps us to understand local studies in a broader perspective and to build a general framework that includes both the general and the particular levels of understanding. The global perspective helps us to establish the range of human sexual behavior and identify patterns of sexuality connected with other aspects of culture such as religion or economics. A landmark study of sexuality by Clelland Ford and Frank Beach (1951) is a global compilation of sex behavior and attitudes based on a sample of nearly 200 ethnographies of which Malinowski's Trobriand study is one. Cultural comparison is not without its dangers of misuse. For example, in the nineteenth century, amateur anthropologists also did global comparisons by determining how other cultures measured up to European culture. They classified cultures hierarchically, for example, according to whether or not their religion had a single god or many or whether their families were monogamous or polygynous. They chose those characteristics because they considered them to be the key institutions of civilization; they judged the remainder of the world according to these European standards. Because of this systematic bias, they made many mistakes of interpretation. In addition, much of the information they used was itself suspect because it was collected by untrained observers. They did not as a rule use the comparative approach cautiously. When used cautiously, cultural comparison can be enlightening.

The third feature of the anthropological approach is the perspective known as *cultural relativism*. In order to understand this ideal, it is necessary to understand why it was created in the first place. As professional anthropology struggled to be accepted as a legitimate academic discipline in the late nineteenth century it had two important jobs. (1) It had to improve the quality of its information base, and thus it promoted the firsthand study of communities by trained observers. (2) It had to establish some guiding precepts to control the biases that were so characteristic of amateur anthropology in the 1800s. The American version of anthropology in the early twentieth century rejected global comparison because it might bias one's view of a particular culture as it had that of early amateurs, and only later did global cross-cultural studies such as that by Ford and Beach come to be appreciated. Put another way, Boasian (Franz Boas was the founder of American anthropology) anthropology tried to counter comparative bias by saying that each culture must be understood on its own terms and not measured by the standards of others—each culture has its own unique history.

Boasian anthropology then pushed the idea of cultural relativism as a corrective to *ethnocentrism*, the belief that our culture's way is the best and the right way, in fieldwork and cultural comparison. Basically, the precept of cultural relativism is nothing more or less than the familiar social science dictum to study what *is*, rather than what we think should be. In other words, if we want to make judgments, moral or otherwise, at least we should wait until we understand something. Thus, as we encounter various sexual attitudes and practices that we find repugnant across cultures, we need to remember that the first order of scientific business is to find out what is, rather than what we think should be.

We must be careful not to misunderstand cultural relativism to mean that we should enter forever a state of moral neutrality about the customs of other cultures, or that there is no universal human morality and thus anything goes. Instead, we must remember that all cultures have morality from their point of view—morality is a human universal; what is usually at issue is the acceptability of a particular morality to an outsider. In everyday language, we often exclaim that a culture has no morals, when in fact we are saying that it does not have *our* morals. Anthropologists know that a culture is not going to function well without the directive force of a reasonably well accepted and shared moral stance. Large, complex societies will harbor conflicting moralities as is true of the United States today, certainly with respect to sexuality. These conflicts often arise from conditions of change and sometimes threaten social stability as we will see later. Yet, anthropologists also know how easy it is to misunderstand foreign ideas and behaviors, and that makes them wary of making hasty judgments, particularly moralistic ones.

PLAN OF THE BOOK

The goal of this book is simple and straightforward; it offers an essential framework by which to understand human sexuality and from which to launch further inquiries. It does not include all possible topics in cross-cultural sexuality, nor does it explore the many nuances possible on each topic. Specific case studies furnish necessary detail at appropriate points. Chapter 2 establishes the sexual nature of humans in the animal world, the essential nature of humans as creatures highly dependent on learning, and our common biological base. It introduces the concepts of culture and self as basic building blocks for understanding sexuality in different times and places. It discusses the critical ideas of gender, role, and identity, and furnishes a discussion on the importance of systems of meaning and ideas of morality in sexuality.

Chapter 3 opens with a discussion of embodiment, the cultural concept of the body as exemplified in body schemas, genital cutting, tattooing, and blood magic. It introduces romantic passion as a universal experience and examines the topics of beauty and desire. Chapter 4 explores types of sexual behavior and addresses the question of what is normal sexual behavior. It presents the concept of sex patterns and questions standard labels and knowledge of same-sex relationships. This chapter also recognizes the importance of the elements of conflict and change in understanding patterns of sexuality, as illustrated by studies of sex and conquest, sex and slavery, American sexuality, and global sex.

Chapter 5 underscores the key roles of kinship and marriage in shaping sexuality. It emphasizes the importance of economic and political power in controlling sexuality, especially that of women. It deals with the incest taboo, extramarital and premarital sex, and divorce. This chapter also notes the continued decoupling of procreation and sexual intercourse in modern times.

Chapter 6 is devoted to issues in sexuality such as prostitution, pornography, sexual violence, and sexually transmitted diseases. All of these topics raise concerns about standard labels and conceptualizations of sexual phenomena, particularly as evidenced in applied programs against HIV/AIDS in Africa. Chapter 7 offers some concluding remarks and raises questions about the nature of sex in the future.

Chapter Two

Culture, Self, and Sex

Nisa is a !Kung woman (Kalahari Desert in southern Africa) who is telling the anthropologist, Marjorie Shostack (1983), of her youthful struggle with some sexual demands of her culture. In the first passage below she is a young girl resisting playing at sex, and in the second she is not much older but already resisting marriage.

> Another time the boys asked us to play and I said, "Keya and I are going off and play by ourselves. You want to play sexually. Go play your play. But we won't. You want us to do something bad." The boys said, "That's not why! You are going off together so you can screw!" We said, "Not true. Do you think we have penises to have sex with each other with?" "Can two vaginas screw?" The boys said, "You're always playing sexually together. That's why you refuse us." (p. 117)
>
> When I still had no breasts, when my genitals still weren't developed, when my chest was still without anything on it, that was when a man named Bo came from a distant area and people started talking about marriage. Was I not almost a young woman? (p. 133)
>
> One day, my parents and his parents began building our marriage hut. The day we were married, they carried me to it and set me down inside. I cried and cried and cried. Later, I ran back to my parents' hut, lay down beside my little brother, and slept, a deep sleep like death. (p. 133)

In these passages, Nisa is being pressured, in the first instance by playmates and in the second by parents, to do the expected thing. However, she is resisting early sexual experience in a sexually permissive society and retreating from her first marriage, which was appropriately arranged for her in spite of her demonstration of reluctance to marry so young. In spite of her early resistance, and though she continued to see herself as willful, she came eventually to accept many

21

lovers and husbands as a thoroughly !Kung woman would.[1] Her consent pleased her parents.

Nisa's willful behavior invited negative feedback from other !Kung (as demonstrated by the boys' comments) because she was not meeting group expectations. She found this personally painful. Her "culture" asked her to do something she was not prepared emotionally to do yet, but she was pressured to do it anyway. When she did, the negative feedback stopped. She eventually conformed without losing her individuality (Shostak 1983). Nisa simply compromised between her individuality and the demands of the group. By adapting to demands, she found her satisfactions within !Kung culture. On the other hand, her culture did not simply coerce her into conformity, but also supported her by giving her direction and rewarding appropriate behavior.

Nisa's case highlights several inescapable realities in our lives. First, we are biological creatures with certain needs and drives, starting with the simple life-sustaining requirements such as food and water. The sex drive is not necessary for individual survival, but it remains a potent force in human affairs. The second reality is that we are born without choice into a particular culture and society that is already formed. It frustrates us at the same time that it supports us. Third, we are each a conscious, self-aware individual member of a group who must find our own way in the "giveness" of this preformed world. We are reflective, interpretive creatures who attempt to draw meaning from our lives. These realities force a continuing tension between individual needs and goals and those of the group. This strain is the fundamental human condition that applies to all cultural traditions and institutions as well as to human sexuality specifically, as the case of Nisa depicts.

This chapter develops a framework for understanding the individual, social, and cultural dynamics of human sexuality, first by introducing an interactive model of human sexuality that will serve as a general guide in subsequent discussions. Next we explore our basic biological and sexual makeup and then develop the basic concepts of culture and self. Several case studies of how people learn sexuality illustrate the discussions.

AN INTERACTIVE MODEL

In her cross-cultural study of varieties of sexual experience, Suzanne Frayser states:

> If we define human sexuality as a system composed of biological, social, cultural, and psychological attributes that intersect in producing erotic arousal and/or orgasm, and associated with but not

necessarily resulting in reproduction, then it seems to be a perfect topic for anthropological investigation. The interaction among biological, social, cultural and psychological attributes of human sexuality creates a dynamic that makes it possible to study sexuality as an integrated whole rather than a set of loosely connected factors. (1999:2)

Frayser advocates a *holistic* view of sexuality—the integration of its social, biological, cultural, and psychological attributes—and observes that this is not currently the mainstream anthropological approach (1999:3). A holistic view sees human behavior in as wide a framework as possible, as in placing sexuality in a cultural and historical context. Holism is an old and valued anthropological perspective that is, in fact, not always followed in practice by its practitioners, partly because they too often fragment theoretical issues into smaller, hostile camps (Suggs and Miracle 1999:35). In this competitive environment, the vitality created by dialogue among competing points of view may be lost in the quagmire of hardened positions, and dialogue dies. In pursuing an interactive model, we find soon enough that the study of human sexuality requires in the end an interdisciplinary effort, with plenty of dialogue among competing theories. Taking a holistic view should move those competing camps closer to each other, not farther away.

The implicit model we follow in this text is one that, while underscoring the cultural features of sexuality, accepts the interactive, holistic model proposed by Frayser. The problem with her model and ours is that while they both specify important interactive elements of sexuality, describing and explaining exactly how they interact remains a work in progress. Nevertheless, the goal of integrating these elements in a single model remains desirable even if it is not yet fully achieved. The model here is intended as instructive, not causal.

It depicts the main ingredients that join in forming human sexuality and thus also identifies the foundation of this text. Clearly, both sexual ideals and sexual behavior vary somewhat across cultures, but they also change through history within a single culture, as they have in North American culture. Change alters relationships among the elements of our model (biology, culture, and self) in numerous and important ways.

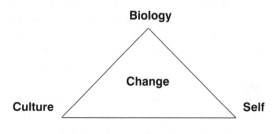

Interactive Model of Sexuality

THE BIOLOGICAL BASE

It is important to establish the biological base by first locating human sexuality in the larger world of sexual reproduction. We will examine five key elements.

1. Sexual reproduction. We are sexually reproducing creatures. In contrast to simple organisms each of which reproduces itself quite efficiently by *binary fission*—that is, by producing an exact copy of itself in what is essentially a cloning procedure—sexual reproduction requires biological males and females. Sexual reproduction appeared about two billion years ago among early single-cell entities and developed in mammals more than 60 million years ago. Sexual reproduction occurs when members of different sexes copulate and male sperm and female egg merge at conception. Copulation is not necessary today, of course, with the availability of high-tech techniques such as in vitro fertilization and artificial insemination.

2. Courtship. Sexual intercourse is preceded by *courtship* during which time and energy is expended in an effort to attract a partner. Courtship in the animal world is usually a case of *male display* and *female choice* of the most worthy candidate. The male peacock spreads a beautiful array of feathers to impress the peahen, who then decides if this display passes the test of fitness. The fitness of a worthy partner can be defined in terms that have survival value. The strongest or healthiest appearing male, for example, would be more highly valued because those qualities will give male offspring of the union a competitive edge in surviving. Darwin called this a process of *sexual selection*, whereby the individuals with the "best" qualities will pass on more (compared to less competitive individuals) and better adapted genetic material to the next generation (although Darwin was unaware of the genetic mechanism by which transmission from one generation to the next took place).

Sexual reproduction may seem to be an inefficient strategy when compared to asexual cloning, because courting requires so much time and energy. But it has the distinct advantage of adding *genetic variety*—the fetus receives half of its genetic material from each parent—to the genetic makeup of the offspring. Genetic diversity permits populations of creatures to be more adaptable to changing environments and circumstances. Less genetic variety in a population of creatures narrows the range of its capacity to respond genetically to changing environments. If there were no long-neck individuals in ancient giraffe populations in East Africa, giraffes would not have survived the climatic change that reduced food sources available to short-neck giraffes. Long-neck giraffes, however, could feed on higher branches of the acacia trees that do well in a more arid environment. As a consequence, only those long-necked individuals with the ability to feed off the higher reaches of acacia trees survive today.

In evolutionary theory, the process of adaptation to an environment is called *natural selection*. In this process, features of the environment—predators, disease, climate change—that exert pressures on living creatures "select" only those individuals in a population who are best fit to survive. Natural selection works at the group, or population, level, while sexual selection works at the individual level; they are two sides of the same coin. While humans are products of natural selection, our success on this planet, paradoxically, is due more to our ability to produce learned solutions to problems of survival than it is due to slow-paced genetic evolution. To possess the intellectual capacity for complex problem solving is itself, of course, a product of our evolution.

Courtship, in evolutionary terms, is an important part of natural selection. Humans may not have natural feathers to display, or engage in courting dances and preening behavior typical of other animals, but we still court and much of our courting behavior is probably due to our own evolutionary past. A number of researchers, for example, have observed flirting patterns of humans, which may be genetically grounded (Eibl-Eibesfeldt 1989).

Courtship, mating strategies, and other issues relating to sexual selection form the centerpiece for much work in sociobiology, or evolutionary psychology as it now known. It focuses heavily on male mating strategies and related topics and reduces the role of culture in shaping human behavior (Buss 1994; Thornhill and Palmer 1999). Although their findings are not particularly robust in support of their arguments, it is important, given our interactive model, to keep open the dialogue about how biology and culture together influence our sexuality.[2]

3. Pair bonding. Sexual reproduction results in extended immaturity, and human offspring experience a longer period of immaturity than other mammals. As a consequence, immature offspring require that one or both parents *invest* in *provisioning* and *protecting* them until they can fend for themselves, thus creating a form of family life. Protecting infants until they are mature and providing them with food is a necessary function for human parents or caretakers. Cooperating parents improve the chances of their offspring to survive to maturity. The parents may be said to *bond* with each other under these conditions for at least some period of time.

4. Continuing sexual receptivity. Humans, however, differ from other creatures (except for their closest living relatives, chimpanzees) in that females are sexually receptive at all times, instead of having *estrus*, a defined period of sexual receptivity that is related to ovulation. Continuous female sexual receptivity influences our sexuality in that considerations other than reproduction come into play. Linda Wolfe (1999:83) suggests that this "permanently sexed" condition underlies definitions of gender roles that also are connected with the sexual division of labor—for example, men hunt and women care for children (Wolfe 1999:83). Being continually sexually receptive, often pregnant, and primarily responsible for child care are attributes that historically combine to support a culturally defined subordinate gender role for women cross-culturally that undermines their access to positions of power and authority. There is nothing about these attributes that inevitably justifies a subordinate role for women, but that is often how cultures have interpreted them.

5. Human sex is more than reproduction. In addition to the fact that we are sexually reproducing creatures is the inescapable fact that sexual reproduction is not the only reason for sexual coupling among humans. Sexual interaction is linked also to play, intimacy, and emotional attachment. These are needs that probably are also a part of our biological makeup as social creatures. These constant and universal features of human sexuality define our capacity in a broad way, but culture shapes the details of local sexual practices around the world.

Setting the biological base of human behavior requires further elaboration of the biological commonality among humans.

1. All humans are of the same species, and our common biological heritage accounts for those universal ways that underlie our behavior regardless of time and place. These constants offer us additional clues to our commonality (Brown 1991). Human groups are not precisely the same, of course, but the point is that genetic and physical differences are minor and rarely bear implications for explaining human behavioral differences (Relethford 2000; Molnar 1983).

2. The brains of all human groups, at birth, are of similar organization and function. The qualifying phrase "at birth" is necessary because there is clear evidence of the interactive nature of the brain, cognition, and experience that can influence the early development and biochemistry of the brain.

3. The human sensory apparatus is everywhere the same. There may be minor differences among populations, but all normal humans have five senses that operate within about the same range of sensitivity. This does not mean that all human groups structure their perceptual world in exactly the same way. If we are raised in an urban environment, we will be unlikely to "read" the forest as well as a lifelong forest dweller who is attuned to its characteristics. But this is a matter of experience and interest not a different sensory capacity.

4. All humans appear to have the same emotional capacity. This does not mean that we all feel necessarily the same way about the same things, but that we all draw on the same emotional range. All normal humans, for example, are capable of some form of love/attachment, anger, and fear.

5. All male humans have the same reproductive system, and all females have the same.

These constants, or universals, define us as a species. At the same time, human ways vary significantly on how they incorporate these constants into culture. The brain is the same for all us, but we do not all structure our reality in the same way. The sex drive is the same for all human groups, but it is managed in ways that vary significantly through historical time and across cultures.

These biological constants are products of our evolutionary development, but brain expansion is the most critical development of all for us. Human evolution is essentially the story of achieving an upright posture, acquiring a larger and more complex brain, and consequently becoming more dependent on learned behavior, or culture. Upright posture preceded brain expansion and is clearly present as early as 3.5 million years ago in a small *hominid* (prehuman) female found in East Africa and given the name of Lucy (Johanson 1981). The fossil record of development in the hominid line to modern humans begins with Lucy and other creatures like her in the same general time period, followed by other upright-striding creatures with small brains and ape-like cranial features (Relethford 2000). Lucy's brain size is about the same as that of a mature chimpanzee. By 500,000 years ago, the time of *Homo Erectus*, the brain size had increased dramatically to reach the lower level of modern humans, and by perhaps 150,000 years ago *Neanderthal* brain capacity matched and sometimes exceeded that of modern humans.[3]

Anatomically modern humans appeared at least 40,000 or more years ago. Giving birth to a large-brain offspring would present an enormous danger to the health of both a "modern" mother and child because a mature, large-brain head would be too large to pass easily, without damage, through the average birth canal. The evolutionary solution appears to have been to permit the child to be born with a small brain that would grow postnatally to its mature size. During its long period of immaturity, where the brain does not reach its full potential until the age of 12 to 14 years, the human offspring is learning what anthropologists call culture. Culture is the primary way in which human groups adapt to the world. The individual's success in a culture depends in large measure on his or her learning to be a competent adult during the long period of maturation.

LEARNING A CULTURE

Culture refers to behavior, values, and attitudes. Culture is *learned*. The roots of the word culture (from the Latin verb *colere*) refer to cultivation (Wagner 1975:21). Thus, we nurture infants; we grow them to maturity. While growing up, children learn language, practical skills, values, meanings, emotions, and knowledge. They learn about themselves in terms of gender, identity, and role. Successful cultural adaptations require a secure and detailed knowledge of their environment, whether urban or rural, that can best be learned by a long and involved experience with it. Survival skills include the ability to observe, remember, and communicate. Children in tropical forest environments can name and identify hundreds of native plants and know the habits of many animals. If children grow up in a city they will learn the ways of the city rather than those of the country.

Culture is *shared* among the members of a society, thus enhancing cooperation and coordination of individual effort toward social goals. Children grow up learning in social contexts and eventually accepting, as did Nisa, the values and goals of the group. This is a process of *enculturation*. Learning a language is critical to acquiring culture because it is the fundamental vehicle for bearing, using, and sharing culture. When members of a society accept the core values and goals of the group, they are more likely to cooperate with each other, thereby reducing internal conflict and dispute. A system of rewards and punishments supports the core culture. In addition, humans everywhere must secure a living, form families, make group decisions, defend themselves, and deal with internal conflict. These activities are handled by the group as a matter of shared culture. These features among others are universals, but they vary in their details from culture to culture.

Because the knowledge and skills of one generation can be transmitted to the next, culture is *accumulative*. Human groups can thus refine their adaptations to their environment through the generations as their knowledge accumulates and their skills improve. The domestication of plants and animals took place over numerous generations and could develop only because the knowledge of one generation was transmitted to the next, and thus the same lessons did not have to be learned anew by each succeeding generation. The ability to pass on information to the next generation gives culture *continuity* through the generations.

Culture is *socially learned*; it can be learned only in the presence of other humans. In fact, the lack of significant contact with other humans severely interferes with the learning process so that, in extreme cases of individual isolation, nothing at all is learned.[4] Thus the *ca-*

pacity to learn a culture is given to every normal human as a matter of genetic inheritance, but culture can actually be acquired only by social learning. The learning process is based on a combination of techniques such as observation, imitation, experimentation, and direct instruction. Acquiring practical skills, rules of social interaction, and a host of other seemingly ordinary daily behaviors, including sexuality, is always accompanied by attitudes and values. For example, perhaps a field should not be plowed unless one first offers prayers to the spirits to insure a good harvest. When we say that sex should only be practiced for the purpose of reproduction, we are attaching a value to sexual behavior.

Maturing children *internalize* the lessons of their culture so well and so deeply that most of the lessons persist for their entire life span. This is the primary reason that even professionally trained anthropologists sometimes find it difficult to see objectively through their own cultural screen as they observe another culture. By the time they train as anthropologists, they already carry with them considerable cultural baggage accumulated since childhood. To internalize means that we take our culture for ourselves, commit to it, and become dedicated carriers of that culture. The way we see the world, the way we feel about things, the way we interact with others in our group, these are all learned in particular ways. Moreover, internalization means that most of our cultural learning is enacted unconsciously. We do not often examine our routine behavior unless attention is drawn to it for some unusual reason at which time we become more conscious of our learned ways. As noted earlier, learning a culture does not eliminate our individuality. However, we can only form a personality and a selfhood in a cultural context, and during the process we will learn to compromise our individuality with group demands.

Culture is *adaptive*. Learning is the predominant way in which humans survive under changing conditions. The importance of learned skills continues to grow in our increasingly technological age, further underscoring its importance. The idea of adaptation is sometimes misunderstood to mean that a group of culture-bearing people (a society) learns the very best way of adapting to an environment, but in fact the level of adaptation needs only to be minimally successful—successful enough to insure survival through generations under a given set of conditions. Each culture produces some behavior (values, attitudes, actions) that could be seen as *maladaptive* or potentially so, but they generally are not a serious enough problem to prevent adaptation to stable conditions. Some behavior is neutral; it doesn't help and it doesn't hurt. Whether or not behavior is adaptive or maladaptive depends mostly on the nature of any changes in the environment. Because the concept of adaptation was first widely applied to biological evolutionary problems, it invokes thoughts of creatures surviving against predators in a natural habitat. For humans (and increasingly so for other creatures of the world), the natural environment includes coping with the nearby presence of other humans. The environment to which we adapt is then both natural and social.

Specific cultural adaptations may have consequences for sexuality. For example, after a nation has fought a war costly in human lives, it might place a renewed emphasis on producing replacement offspring; this was the case in Europe between the world wars (Altman 2001:62). Some nations, such as China, want to reduce population growth and have instituted birth control measures as a matter of national policy. In an ethnic conflict, one group might forbid sex and marriage of its members with those of the other group in order to preserve cultural boundaries and maintain "purity." Many cultures that seek to exert control over female fertility and reproduction also seek to limit premarital and extramarital sexual access to women. It will be seen later that strict measures aimed at controlling female fertility are generally associated with certain kinds of cultures operating under certain conditions of adaptation. These adaptations do not necessitate such strict control over sex, but it is an integral part of some nevertheless.

Being raised in a culture that we have internalized so deeply and enact so habitually sets us up for the condition of *culture shock*. Culture shock arises when we are made conscious of our culture by its contrast with the ways of another culture. We may have some trouble getting past our own way of seeing and doing things and therefore experience problems functioning in the new culture. Specifically, culture shock *occurs when we are having difficulty dealing with an alien way of life*. While outsiders' reactions to a given culture vary widely, some common symptoms of culture shock are irritability, depression, withdrawal, paranoia, and alcohol abuse (Ferraro 2001:98–99). Culture shock can range from severe to mild, occur over a short or long period of time, and strike more than once. Culture shock reminds us of how bound we are by our own culture and how difficult it is to break its bounds. Nevertheless millions of people do live successfully and comfortably in cultures in which they were not raised. Anthropologists expect culture shock and use it to their advantage by treating it as an additional tool to help them understand their own culture as well as the new culture.

So comfortable do we become with our culture that other ways of life may appear to us to be unnatural or somehow wrong. This is a condition known as ethnocentrism (a concept introduced in chapter 1), being centered in our own lifeway. Ethnocentrism and culture shock are closely related in that they both speak of difficulty in dealing with cultures and groups that are different. Ethnocentrism occurs on several levels. An *explicit ethnocentrism* is a frank dislike for and unwillingness to try to understand another culture. There is nothing hidden about this antipathy; it is openly acknowledged. An *implicit ethnocentrism*, however, is that deep, hidden ethnocentrism that is difficult to know about until it has been challenged by cultural differences. It lurks in our unconsciousness. For example, some anthropologists have been writing recently about a deep-seated Western bias based on giving priority to visual experience (Stoller 1997). They see Western science as based on "observation" and similar visual metaphors. Thus, anthropologists do participant *observation*.

Our modern technological life depends much on visual data displays, lately reinforced by widespread computer use. Sexuality in America is heavily visual as represented by our immersion in mass media, especially television and videotape. As a consequence, sound, touch, and odor are reduced in significance. Yet many other cultures accentuate these other senses, for example in the natural sounds of the forest or the taste of food. Has anthropology in its embrace of Western science missed the potential importance of other senses in their studies of other cultures because of this heretofore unrecognized bias? Critics such as Paul Stoller (1997) have made a good case that anthropology has succumbed to this ethnocentrism. If one is unable to overcome the limits of one's own culture, then it becomes difficult to see other cultures in an unbiased light, thus leading to misunderstanding and misjudgment. The example of sensory bias illustrates how difficult it can be even for trained observers to get at those deep, underlying biases formed when we were young and reinforced through our many years of maturation.

CULTURE, COGNITION, AND EMOTIONS

It is important for our future discussion to examine briefly the interplay of culture, cognition, and emotions, because doing so illustrates how deeply cultural learning penetrates our being and explains why we are so culture-bound *Cognition* refers to our ability to manipulate and use information. It includes making choices, constructing mental categories, planning, and problem solving—in short, our higher intellectual processes. Cognitive capacity is much the same for all normal humans because it is based on the same brain structure and neurochemical processes characteristic of our species. Language is a key cognitive function, but as variable as are the thousands of languages that exist in the world, they all operate within the same general framework, and vary from each other in limited ways (Chomsky 1957). Yet, these small variances make languages mutually unintelligible to each other. Fortunately, they can be learned by anyone under proper circumstances because they are all human languages with a common base. There are no inferior languages or cultures. They do whatever they are designed to do in the contexts in which they exist.

This text contains numerous examples of how we cognitively structure sexuality. Cultures, for example, construct different mental images of the process of conception and gestation of the fetus, a process that is invisible in ordinary daily life. These images, or conceptualizations, form what is called a *schema*.[5] A schema is a mental picture that organizes information into usable units. Thus various groups may construct different schemas about what is going on inside a pregnant woman. A common schema of conception in preliterate cultures is that the semen of the man and the blood of the woman join to form the fetus and that additional deposits of semen are necessary to nourish its growth in the womb. Modern science, of course, presents a quite different schema involving fertilization and gestation. A schema includes ideas and explanations about events and processes unseen, such as conception and gestation, as well as classifying and mentally connecting visible objects. For example, indigenous Amazonian people construct schemas about which plant in the jungle has medicinal uses for a given illness, or they build a mental map of the network of local trails running through the rainforest.

Do all humans have the same emotions? Yes, and no. Consistent with the perspective we have developed so far, it is assumed that we all have the same *emotional capacity* that we inherit as members of the same species. Yet, these emotional capacities are so shaped and nuanced by culture that they become fundamental sources of misunderstanding and stereotyping between groups. Once again we are faced with the daunting task of balancing on the one hand our human similarities and on the other the profound differences we can develop through our different lived experiences (Middleton 1998). In general, we are compelled by cross-cultural evidence (Ekman 1973) to assume that all humans share general emotion states, such as joy, anger, fear, disgust, surprise, attachment, and loss. Beyond these basic states, how many emotions we have becomes a naming game, and the more emotions we name, the more difficult it becomes to demonstrate their universality.

To assume, however, that all humans have the same emotions carries certain dangers. While the assumption speaks to our commonality across cultures, it might lead one to the false conclusion that emotions are used in the same way and bear the same meaning in another culture that they do in one's own culture. It is accurate to grant all humans the same emotional capacity as members of the same species, but the matter does not end there. Emotional states are patterned and entwined in the fabric of the local culture. Indeed, part of what a culture does is to manage our individual emotional lives. That is, it establishes understandings about what to get angry or happy about and how and when to express those emotions. In one culture a death is mourned, while in another death brings expressions of happiness. Being joyful at a relative's death would strike most Westerners as bizarre, but others might consider Western mourning habits just as bizarre.

Emotional expression is managed by the group and by self-monitoring individuals who have acquired a set of cultural norms and values. In the West, we tend to think of emotions as distinctly individual; after all we feel them intensely in our bodies and minds, and our cultural focus on individualism supports this thought. But emotions are not ours alone; they are also social. This is why many anthropologists studying emotions focus on *emotional expression* as the social self interacts in situations and relationships, rather than on deep individual emotional structures as Freud did (although that approach remains an option). Because we share consistent, normative understandings about emotional expression, we can think of cultures as containing *emotional styles* (Middleton 1989). When the people of one culture publicly joke and have fun with sexuality, and the people of another culture are reluctant to mention sexuality and find no joy in it, the two represent different emotional understandings of sexuality. These understandings are part of their emotional style. Cognitive schema and emotional styles are part of our adaptation to the challenges of our local environment. Thinking and feeling are tailored to the needs of humans everywhere, and that is why these patterns need to be understood in their context.

SELF, GENDER, AND ROLE

Learning a culture transforms the raw potential of the newborn into a social person and a culturally competent adult. Children who do not have this transforming experience are left in a severely disadvantaged condition. In severe cases of isolation, they learn nothing and thus become nothing but creatures who need to satisfy their basic drives. Without a language they cannot communicate, and they form no self-concept. Consequently, they learn nothing of social roles and identities and are unlikely ever to become competent adults. Although they may eventually masturbate to experience a pleasant sensation and they will satisfy the requirements of survival with food and drink, sex roles, gender identification, and sexuality have no significance to them. They remain unformed and incomplete.

The self is a socially aware person who adjusts behavior as he or she encounters and interprets different social contexts.[6] We all have both a relatively invisible private life and a visible public one. The *social interactionist* approach to the concept of self targets the public and adaptive behavior of individuals operating in everyday contexts.[7]

It avoids a more psychologically oriented concept of self, such as a focus on personality, which depends on techniques designed to get at the deep psychological processes of individuals as in dream analysis, a Rorschach (inkblot) test, or psychoanalysis. Both the social interactionist and psychological approaches make an arbitrary and artificial distinction between outer and inner life—a distinction that does not exist in reality—in order to focus more directly on one aspect. The *social interactionist* perspective does not claim that the psychological approach is wrong, only that much knowledge about the self can be gained by observing our social actions.

To gain a better understanding of the idea behind the presentation of self, we might imagine ourselves in three different contexts—classroom, student party, home—and ask a simple question. Are we the same person in all three contexts, mostly the same person, or radically different? We likely will conclude that we modify our behavior at least somewhat in each of these settings, because we play different roles in different contexts—a student in the classroom, a friend or date at the party, a family member at home. Yet we are not fundamentally a different person in any of these contexts. Contextual variations in performance simply reveal different facets of our self; they are part of our ability to present our self as the occasion warrants. Goffman (1959) used the term *impression management* to get at this tendency to vary our public performance.

Presenting our self appropriately in different situations depends on the cognitive/emotional act of properly *interpreting* the social and emotional meaning of the context so that we can act accordingly. How does a given situation fit into our personal cognitive schema? The interpretation is partly emotional because of our past experiences and expectations associated with the context and what they meant to us previously. In other words, we have an emotional as well as a cognitive memory that influences our perceptions and interpretations. The classroom, the party, and the home contexts have different emotional implications for us. We are essentially asking: what does this situation mean for who I think I am as a social person; what role is required; what presentation of my self do I make? Much of life is routine, of course, and so we all move routinely through a variety of contexts—home, work, play—where we lapse habitually into learned roles and behaviors. Yet, even in this habitual round of activity a person is still a conscious, interpreting self, who might have to deal with an attack on his/her self-concept, with changes in the tasks associated with a role, or even with a fundamental redefinition of a role.

Wikan (1990) writes persuasively about the complex reality behind the bright face of the Balinese. The Balinese think of themselves as participating in the drama of life but certainly not as unidimensional characters. The public image of the Balinese in the Western world is one of a group of people who are poised and graceful at all times, in even the fine details of their daily life. But there is more here than meets the eye. Women are particularly concerned with displaying a bright face at all times. Indeed, others judge them on their ability to make people feel at ease by not revealing the conflicts and negative emotions that might be hidden behind their bright face. Although men are not as harshly judged as women, they, too, are expected to exercise control over their emotional expression. The Balinese emphasize managing and concealing turbulent hearts in times of loss and pain, and each person knows very well the tremendous effort it takes to manage the heart. It is part of their emotional style. The Balinese justify their emphasis on public composure on the basis of morality.

We form a *self-concept*, a mental image of ourselves, that is composed of (1) past experiences, (2) the meaning we attach to those experiences, and (3) what others think of us. To expand on the latter point, learning who we are as a person, a self, depends in a substantial way on how others react to us. We may or may not agree or accept their assessment, but it is in this interaction with others that we form a self-concept. Nisa's self-concept was that she was still a child, but her parents married her to a man in the belief that it was time for her to become an adult. Because of her recalcitrance, Nisa formed the image of herself as difficult and resistant, willful, an image reinforced by the opinions of others. A self-concept guides our behavior and gives it some consistency from context to context. Thus, the contextual flexibility of a person suggested by the definition of the self as interpretive and adjusting is balanced by the individual consistency and continuity that normally characterizes our life course.

The idea of self fits well with the notion of individual adaptation to social life. As cultures adapt to their environment, so do individuals adapt to their culture. By examining the adapting self, we are able to see better how individuals adjust their behavior, plans, and goals in changing circumstances. Of key importance in this respect is to define from the individual's point of view what specific aspects of the environment require a response and what that response would be. In times of economic and culture change, would an individual choose to migrate to the city, seek more education, or become a prostitute? What choices are available to the person from his or her point of view? Other social characteristics such as gender, age, or social status also influence individual action. Cultural conceptions of self, role and status define us as social individuals in a particular culture. As such, they provide us with prescriptions for thought and action and govern everyday traffic in social interaction.

Culture establishes guidelines for *normative* behavior, that is, the range of expected and accepted behavior of individuals as members of a society. Expected behavior is made even more specific by various specific *social roles*—for example, parent, teacher, or police officer. A person does not mature simply as an anonymous member of a society, but as a particular kind of a social person, or self. We all acquire in our lives a set of specific identities, roles, and statuses that guide our behavior. A social status is a position in the social structure, which may be ranked higher or lower than other positions within that structure. In the United States, the role of a bank president carries a higher status than the role of mother. A social role *prescribes* the appropriate behavior that a person occupying a particular status should display and *proscribes* inappropriate behavior. The status of parent carries with it certain rights and duties for those individuals occupying that status. A person's failure to live up to role expectations invites *sanctions* against that person. Some roles and statuses are *ascribed* at birth such as gender or royalty, while others such as Ph.D. or M.D. are *achieved* by learning to play the role successfully according to set standards and receiving, as a result, recognition of that achievement. However, different individuals perform roles, within limits, somewhat differently. We might be actors in real life playing roles and following a cultural script already written for us, but we bring to these roles, as do actors on stage, our individual interpretations.

Roles provide us with guidelines for social interaction and a partial definition of the self. Teachers and students have a range of predefined behaviors and attitudes that guide their interaction on the school premises. Often testing the boundaries of what is considered appropriate behavior in a role, for example the occurrence of sexual behavior between student and instructor, will generate sanctions against such behavior should it become public knowledge. Roles and statuses are ways of socially locating people and this is important because they carry with them assumptions about attitudes, values, and behavior.

Roles and statuses change as culture changes, creating *role conflicts* and *role strain*. In role conflict, a person experiences conflicts among the role expectations, and role strain raises the possibility of not meeting all expectations. The expectations of the roles, mother and/or wife may come into conflict with career aspirations. This expanded definition of what it means to be a woman in contemporary society contains conflicts that create a strain on fulfilling the role. We all, of course, play multiple roles, and sometimes it is difficult to give them all sufficient attention in today's busy and complex life. Culture change challenges old values and expectations. An individual in these ambiguous circumstances may become uncertain about how to act properly in spite of being motivated to do so. In the United States in the 1960s, the women's movement not only advocated women's rights but demanded as well a different definition of a woman's role, and consequently a man's role, in the home and marriage. This transformation included altering attitudes about women's reproductive role and fostering a more aggressive female sexuality. Under the pressure of change, many women and men became confused about their roles and selves and were uncertain about what behavior should guide their interaction with each other.

For most of history and in every culture, biological sexual identity has defined a *master role* for men and women (although some cultures do not limit the possibilities to this dyad) that carries with it broad consequences for their behavior. A master role is an overarching role definition from which other roles derive. For example, in many cultures, the master role for women defines them as generally passive, whether in politics, economics, or sexuality, while men are given more active roles. Women by this cultural definition are generally confined to the domestic sphere, a subordinate status, and a passive sexuality, while men take the public, dominant, and active role. Gender definition, then, is often a master role that entails a host of assumptions about division of labor, power, authority, and sexuality. In practice, women often resist their master role and fashion more assertive roles. The feminist wave in the 1960s was aimed at showing how arbitrary this culturally defined master role is for women.

One of the principal challenges we face as social creatures is to bring the individual into line with prevailing cultural norms and values. Much of the foregoing discussion clarifies how this alignment is achieved, although of course it is an imperfect process. A convenient way to think about this challenge is to imagine a culture as a way of making plans and setting goals for the general good, and guiding its members' behavior toward realizing them. Once individuals accept and internalize these plans and goals, they become competent, culture-sharing, self-monitoring adults. One byproduct of this enculturation process is that deeply ingrained habits are sometimes difficult to change when necessary. Change is often too uncomfortable and even painful for us to consider, but sometimes we must discard or modify old habits of thought and action in order to adapt to new challenges. Much of human conflict is found in this complex tension at the intersection of tradition and change, individual and group.

Regardless of effective enculturation, humans clearly remain individuals to a degree. Therefore, it might be useful to conceive of enculturation as an internalization of culture and an *organization of individual differences* (Wallace [1961]1970:23). Different personalities may adhere to cultural norms and play socially defined roles in a variety of ways but within acceptable limits. Their presentation of self may be quite similar, but not identical. Individuals internalize lessons of enculturation yet remain somewhat unique. Enculturation is not an all-powerful cloning process. Therefore, an effective culture is one that organizes these differences with reasonable success so that work gets done and the culture continues.

LEARNING SEXUALITY

Humans learn sexuality. While the sex drive is the same for all human groups (individuals may vary in its strength), it must be channeled and directed by learned behavior; its disruptive potential must be reduced by social values and practices that direct sexual energy toward socially defined goals. As individuals we learn what kind of sexual creatures we are as we learn gender roles and acquire cultural guidelines regarding such elements of sexuality as desirability, courtship, foreplay, and sexual positions. One of the assumptions made by those who study sexuality is that laws and customs are one thing, but individual behavior is another. Nevertheless, the enculturation process is a powerful one, and individuals do not easily cast off its effects. The following examples of learning sexuality will provide us with some examples that highlight the processes we have discussed in this chapter.

Trobriand sexuality (Malinowski [1929]1987) is characterized by a great amount of sexual freedom starting early in life. The choices of sexual partners is wide and the opportunities to satisfy sexual desire numerous for both genders. Trobriand children are generally given a great deal of freedom and begin to form small groups independent of their parents at the age of four or five. They already know something of sexual activity because there is no way for adults to achieve complete privacy, given the open physical structure of the houses in which they live. Adults take no special measures to conceal sexual talk or acts. The children thus learn at an early age how to talk and joke about sex and have many opportunities to observe the act. The children initiate each other into erotic matters, although the incest taboo holds even at that age for brothers and sisters. Oral and manual manipulation of sexual organs is the most common experience in the earlier years. Soon older children allow younger ones to observe them in sexual acts. Sexual themes also are part of many of the games that they play, although boys and girls usually play apart as their gender identity and role playing begin to develop. Adults take little interest in the sexual explorations of their children.

In adolescence, sexuality begins to change. Between the ages 12 and 14, boys begin to mature physically and to leave the home so as not to hamper the sexual activity of their parents. The youths enter a bachelor's hut, called the *bukumatula*. Girls also leave to live in the house of a relative. Neither gender has much responsibility at this time and is free to pursue fun and pleasure. The youths arrange picnics and excursions in order to meet and frequently make sexual connections with counterparts in other villages. At this point, the short experimental erotic encounters become more serious and longer lasting, but the "love affairs" of adolescents are still free and not totally binding. Yet, as time passes, they form more permanent relationships with the potential for marriage. A serious commitment, however, does not curtail other sexual adventures, which are now reduced in number. In this stage, a more permanent couple may reside with four or five similarly committed couples in the *bukumatula*. There is no legal obligation between the two; they are linked only by passion and personal ties. The couple shares only their bed.

Among the Canela of the Amazon (Crocker and Crocker 1994), boys and girls learn about sexuality early by a variety of means. Sexual contact is defined as generosity and enacted and discussed in the context of fun and joy. There are extramarital trysts, ceremonial sex, and sequential sex as well as adolescent experimentation. Children learn values and attitudes regarding sex simply by being around when adults are speaking. They hear the noises and rustling of sexual activity emanating from sleeping platforms in the house. Classificatory aunts and nephews, and uncles and nieces, enjoy sexual jokes and roughhouse. Females grab at penises and males try to suck female breasts. All of this is done, however, in the company of others and not to the point of physical or emotional pain. In public ceremonies, men and women joke and mimic sexuality. A woman might don male clothing and a specially decorated gourd representing a penis, which she wears belted around her waist, to the enjoyment of all. Thus boys and girls mature in an atmosphere that fosters and values sexuality and prepares them for their own sexual experiences. Nevertheless, when virginal girls have their first sexual intercourse, they are considered to be engaged to the boy. Alternatively, they might become engaged first and then engage in sexual intercourse.

Between about 12 and 17 years of age, youth are free to experiment sexually. A girl can participate in traditional ceremonial and extramarital (although she is unmarried) sexual affairs. Upon marriage she must within several months begin to have sex with her "other" husbands (her husband's male kinsmen). Although there is occasionally a girl who has difficulty doing this, she is accused of being stingy, and will be brought around eventually to perform her duty. A number of her husband's kinsmen may appear at the house one day when he is out hunting, and she knows that sex with them will follow. Some Canela ceremonies require that women retire to the bush for sequential sex with a number of unrelated men. Although expected and usually enjoyed by the women, every eligible woman does not necessarily participate each time.[8]

Boys are equally exposed to the sexual banter as they grow up. Bands of them may roam about looking for women with whom to experiment, but not for the purpose of penetration. Once adolescent boys accumulate some sexual experience they are required to take part in ceremonial and sequential sex associated with the wild boar ceremony. Although women are encouraged and pressured by socialization not to be stingy, in fact they have latitude in choosing not to participate at a particular ceremony. To the contrary, the boys are absolutely required to participate. They have no choice. After they reach their social maturity (in their late teens), however, their sexual attendance at such ceremonies is no longer compulsory.

In this seemingly permissive culture, masturbation is forbidden for both sexes. Indeed, boys and girls are not left alone much and have little chance to masturbate. They are encouraged to have heterosexual experience early and often, and being alone is considered to be stingy and self-indulgent in a culture that stresses the greater good of the group. To what extent masturbation actually takes place is unknown, but it is probably rare because heterosexual contact is readily available (Crocker and Crocker 1994).

The Trobrianders and the Canela could be described as sex-positive cultures in Vern Bullough's (1976) terms. The opposite is true of what has been called an Irish folk community, an island named Inis Beag (Messenger 1969). In contrast to the Trobrianders and the Canela, there is no joking or joy in sex in this Irish community. Sex is not a topic of conversation, and the sexes are kept separate from an early age and segregated in almost all public gatherings, including church. Their understanding of the physical side of sexuality is quite limited. Boys get their information from older boys and from observing animals. There appears to be no "dirty joke" tradition. There is no premarital sex, but males masturbate. When it comes time to marry, there has been almost no sexual experience on either side, and coition appears to be male initiated, almost without foreplay, and with some clothing still on. The sex-negative messages are as clear to them as the positive ones are to the Canela.

Today in the United States, child rearing with respect to sexuality is quite variable. If the poll information cited at the beginning of this book is reasonably accurate, much of the sex education of our youth comes from television and from age mates, who also watch television. Formal sex education in school is more or less explicit, depending on the school district (Irvine 2000). Families vary greatly in their attitudes toward sex and their willingness to discuss it with children, depending on their religion, education, and politics (Lauman, Gagnon, Michael, and Michaels 1994). A number of variables in the United States, a complex society, affect sex education; among them are social class, religious affiliation, and ethnicity. It is quite difficult to judge how much actual sexual experimentation goes on among youth in the United States, because, like most human sexual activity, it takes place out of sight. Surveys depend greatly on self-reporting, resulting in varying degrees of accuracy.

SUMMARY

Human sexuality emerges from the interaction of culture, self, and biology. These elements form the inescapable realities of our existence. Our sexual drive needs to be culturally managed, because it is potentially disruptive of group life. Integrating and coordinating sexual expression in a reasonably consistent way at both group and individual levels remains one of the critical tasks facing humans. The task is accomplished largely through the acquisition of culture—the process of enculturation. Culture change further complicates the goal of forming a consistent lifeway by shifting goals and redefining means by which to meet them. As sexually reproducing creatures we seek mates through courtship. If courtship is successful, we bond with the mate. The constant sexual receptivity of females makes it possible to have sex for intimacy and play as well as for reproduction. This "permanently sexed" condition, however, also lends support to a culturally defined master gender role for women and men, which is not biologically determined.

All human groups share a common biological base—for most of us our brains and our sensory and reproductive systems function the same way, and we have the same general emotional capacity. All competent humans must learn a culture, which as social creatures, we share with others. We internalize a culture so early in our lives that we enact it routinely and unconsciously on a daily basis. It is our capacity to accumulate knowledge that gives us the adaptive power to thrive in diverse environments. Learning a culture necessarily means learning the self, role, and status to which more specific everyday behaviors are attached, including sexuality. Learning a culture, however, sets us up for culture shock and ethnocentrism, both resulting from difficulty in handling emotionally and intellectually the differences we observe in other cultures. We can learn to use culture shock to understand ourselves better.

CRITICAL INQUIRY

1. Try to imagine what our lives would be like if we engaged in sex only to produce offspring. What would human relationships be like? What about art, literature, or drama? What kind of relationship would we have with our children?

2. Can you identify characteristics of yourself formed by your family, gender, or culture? What part of you do you think is fairly unique to you?

3. Can you define the character of your sexual learning? What have you learned about sexuality (sexual anatomy, values, and attitudes) and how did you learn it?

NOTES

---

[1] The !Kung are classified as hunters and gatherers; they do not own property and therefore usually do not impose strict rules on extramarital affairs or divorce. (See chapter 5 for further explanation.)

[2] Critical responses to evolutionary psychology can be found in Caulfield (1985).

[3] Some experts are now suggesting that Neanderthals might have formed a side branch on the tree of human evolution and not on the main trunk line to us.

[4] The critical importance of learning is underscored by the fact that children who are severely isolated from human contact may mature physically without being true humans in the sense that they can't speak, or walk, and know nothing of themselves except as a creature with basic needs to survive. Under these conditions offspring are not likely to achieve their full genetic potential in terms of physical stature or intelligence. Even under remedial instruction they never catch up to the appropriate level and usually die young. As a result of negative early experiences, brain function can fall well short of its initial potential.

[5] See de Munck 2000 for a detailed discussion of different kinds of schemas.

[6] See de Munck 2000 for a succinct history of the development of the concept.

[7] The social interactionists emerged under the influence of G. H. Mead (1968) and Erving Goffman, especially in the latter's *The Presentation of Self in Everyday Life* (1959).

[8] Crocker and Crocker (1994) cite an example of a wife's reluctance to have sex with kinsmen and a husband's jealousy over sharing his wife's sexual services.

Chapter Three

The Sexual Body

A Trobriand *tabula*, a woman who is sexually and maritally taboo to a particular young man, is applying ceremonial dressing, cosmetics, to him so that he may dance in a ceremony of beauty magic. As
she strokes the man's face she speaks the following words to him:

Who makes the beauty magic?
To heighten the beauty, to make it come out.
Who makes it on the slopes of Obukula?
I, Tabula, and my mate Kwaywaya.
We make the beauty magic.
I smooth out, I improve, I whiten!
Thy head I smooth out, I improve, I whiten!
Thy cheeks I smooth out, I improve, I whiten!
Thy nose I smooth out, I improve, I whiten!
Thy throat I smooth out, I improve, I whiten!
Thy neck I smooth out, I improve, I whiten!
Thy breast I smooth out, I improve, I whiten!
Bright skin, bright; glowing skin, glowing.

(Malinowski [1929]1987:208–9)

The purpose of the beauty magic ceremony is to make a man
". . . erotically, irresistible to some one member of the opposite sex"
(p. 291). Contained in this formula is both a concept of male beauty
and an effort to influence the course of mutual attraction with words
and cosmetics. It is also a ritual. Malinowski notes that the formula
must be recited directly to the man's face. By this ritual, Trobrianders take cultural control of the body, just as humans have done
throughout the world from ancient times.

This chapter examines two central and related questions. First,
how do we transform the "natural body" into a social and cultural en-

43

tity? Second, how within this general process do we make the body sexual? The section on learning sexuality in chapter 2 points us in the right direction as we consider these questions, because learning sexuality necessarily involves learning attitudes and values about the body and its functions. We can observe the imprint of culture in other ways too, such as male and female circumcision, blood magic, and body piercing. Still other embodiments are manifest in notions of desire, beauty, and romantic passion. We consider all of these topics in this chapter. It is most important, though, to begin with the first question about the general process of transforming the body into a social and cultural product.

EMBODIMENT

This chapter addresses the body as a presence to be managed and explained. All cultures have "body issues" with which they must deal. Beauty magic is a ritual statement about certain physical attributes being more attractive than others, and about using cosmetics to enhance those attributes. Malinowski writes about the sense of modesty that guides movement and posture among the scantily clad Trobriand islanders. Taboos regarding menstrual blood and initiation rites involving the modification of sexual organs are body issues. They are body issues, not because they are controversial among the members of a culture, but because they are singled out for special cultural attention. They are "commented" on in ritual and in everyday language. All cultures construct schema about the significance of the body and its functions, and how it fits into their way of life. Body schema and body issues are a part of *embodiment*.

To embody is to seize the body culturally. By this concept social scientists seek to understand how cultures address the fact of our physical presence and its meaning; *it sees the body as a social and cultural product.* Embodiment joins the self with the body and places them both in a specific historical and cultural context. Further, "embodiment reminds us of the here-and-now presence of people to one another and the full complement of senses and feelings through which they communicate with one or another" (Strathern 1996). The body has margins and orifices. It is decorated, pierced, and otherwise modified; it works, plays, and performs ritual. It has sex. The body's daily care and activity is guided culturally by our learned intentions and habits.

The French sociologist, Marcel Mauss ([1935]1973:75, cited in Lock 1993) notes that the body was probably the "first and most natural instrument" to receive the imprint of culture. The archaeological record clearly supports Mauss's statement as it richly documents ancient body adornment and alteration. But given our disposition to organize our experience and to assign meaning to it, this record should not surprise us. How could we as cultural creatures avoid intellectually and emotionally addressing the fact of our physical existence? Mauss had in mind, however, something more subtle and elusive than enlarged lips, ear plugs, bones through the nose, and a complete body tattoo, although they certainly qualify. It is Mauss who, in his concept of *habitus*, invites us to take a fresh look at how our most fundamental everyday activity is directed by social rules. By habitus he intends to identify those habits of the body that we perform daily but unconsciously for the very reason that they are habitual. Eating, drinking, eliminating body wastes, having sex, menstrual flow, and semen emissions are natural processes that recede into our unconsciousness because they are "natural" and habitual. But they are also cultural and social. Social scientists like Mauss and Malinowski argue that the power of society and culture form and guide human behavior in fundamental ways. What better proof of their argument but to show how these fundamental and natural bodily functions are culturally managed. In their view, both the body and the person are, in today's theoretical terms, socially and culturally "constructed."

Mary Douglas (1966), takes the body to be a symbol of society. Trained in the British structural function tradition, she was already prepared to make an analogy between the body as a complex system of bony structures and organ functions and the more invisible structures and functions of society. Therefore she emphasizes the importance of the body as a concrete image for more intangible ideas. Because society is an abstraction, we can, in effect, give it "living tissue" through an *organic analogy* with the body. The way in which the institutions of society are related integrally with each other resembles the structure—the skeleton—of the body, while the institutions individually are analogous to body organs providing the necessary functions to sustain life.

> The body is a model that can stand for any bounded system. Its boundaries can represent any boundaries which are threatened or precarious. The body is a complex structure. The functions of its different parts and their relation afford a source of symbols for other complex structures. We cannot possibly interpret rituals concerning excreta, breast milk, saliva and the rest unless we are prepared to see in the body a symbol of society, and to see the powers and dangers credited to social structure reproduced in small on the human body. (Douglas 1966:2)

Douglas's interest in body margins appears especially in her 1966 work, *Purity and Danger*. Building on Mauss's foundation, she focuses on the skin as the social border between person and society. Seeing the body as a natural symbol, she looks at ways in which the margins and functions of the body are thought to be related to social dangers. Substances that enter and exit the body can be dangerous, just as ideas and people that enter or depart a society can be dangerous. Although Douglas develops an anthropology of the body in a series of works, she still does not take into account the full complexity of embodiment. For example, Margaret Lock (1993) notes that any anthropology of the body must include the emotions, which Douglas basically ignores, as well as intellectual elements. Stoller (1997) cautions that the sensuality of the body, its physical essence of sensation and function, is essential to an anthropology of the body.

In her 1993 review of anthropological studies of the body, Margaret Lock notes that it was largely missing, or at least only sporadically visible until the 1970s, in anthropology in spite of the many anthropological studies of human evolution and biological adaptation (see also Burton 2001). One reason for this absence, Lock observes, is that these earlier studies suffered by being outside mainstream anthropological theory. Today there are many studies of the body, from a variety of disciplines, that are better connected to general theoretical developments. The burgeoning study of the body was aided further by feminist scholars, the ethnography of the senses, medical anthropology, and the anthropology of emotions. On the other hand, there is no clear agreement among these lines of thought on how to frame theoretical questions beyond the fact that the body is nowhere culturally insignificant. In general, however, these studies contribute to a new understanding of how we intellectually and emotionally manage the body. These fresh theoretical currents sweep up discourse on the body and propel it into the mainstream of anthropology. Some of these same currents also embrace studies in sexuality, although Lock treats sexuality only tangentially in her review.

Andrew Strathern (1996:196–97) writes that this increase in research on specific bodies actually makes the body as a whole "a silent, unmarked category" entirely dependent for its meaning on other cultural categories. Just as its universal importance as a topic worthy of examination is established and it has become so popular, the body threatens at the same time to disappear again as it is dismembered by various academic specialties (p. 197). It has become the segmented body—a medical body, a consumer body, a gendered body, a sexual body. Perhaps this is the final sense of embodiment—academic cannibalism.

The sexual self is an embodied self. The self is located in a body that has sexual needs, the satisfaction of which is heavily influenced by culture in a particular historical period. Each of us in our subjective experience bears the brunt of whatever tensions and conflicts we experience in a mismatch of sexual needs between self and culture. The history of sexuality in the United States documents the historical shifts in living conditions that resulted in different constructions of sexuality through redefinition of the meaning of marriage, the purpose of sexual intercourse, and the sexual nature of men and women. The body was "re-embodied" in each historical period, challenging individuals to make their adjustments accordingly.

BODY SCHEMA

We are driven by our intellectual and emotional nature to make sense of the world we live in. Classifying, explaining, and valuing are our tools for coping with the world as we find it, and they necessarily include the body's presence. These tools form the core of what is meant by "culturally managing the body," and they are employed to construct a schema of the body. Schemas exist on both individual and cultural levels. Each culture has a body schema (sometimes known as a cultural model at the group level); complex cultures have more than one because of intracultural diversities (class and ethnicity for example). An anthropologist doing research in another culture would have to gain some understanding of that culture's body schema, because it would include not only sexuality, but definitions of routine modesty, personal space, and courtesy as well.

Strathern (1996) describes a schema by which Melanesians connect ideas of morality, sexuality, and the state of one's skin. In examining Melanesian body concepts, Strathern observes that the body is the site of socially defined morality. "The condition of a man's skin therefore is a direct reflection of his current sexual situation" (p. 85). To Melanesians the state of the skin reflects a man's personal and moral state, because they believe that a man ages too quickly if he depletes too much semen. They consider semen to be in short supply. The state of a man's skin then is a result of his own moral choices in life with respect to his sexuality. Most cases of body modification are more obvious than this almost imperceptible skin condition which is not modification at all, but an interpretation of a natural state of the body.

The body can be modified by a number of techniques: (1) substances can be *applied* to the body as in body painting (but other substances like ash or mud can be used); (2) the body can be *inscribed* with cuts (scarification or cicatrization), and if pigment is inserted then it is a tattoo (darker skinned people form decorative welts in the healing process); (3) modification can be accomplished *surgically* as in circumcision, amputation of finger digits, and filing teeth; (4) the essential body can be *shaped* by controlling the growth and shape of the head, neck, or feet; (5) finally, decorative attire can be *worn* to accentuate attractiveness or, again, to indicate one's current social status. The purpose of body modification varies greatly from enhancing one's attractiveness to signifying one's group membership to indicating one's current state—for example, being married or in mourning. Except in rare circumstances, the human body, no matter how unadorned it may seem to be to outsiders, is never naked.

Gregor (1977:154) notes that the Mehinaku (the Brazilian Amazon) are "socially incomplete" if they are naked. They are naked only in special locations or activities such as when they are in their own trash yards, while they are hunting or fishing, and during ceremonies as they move through the life cycle. Body painting and hair dressing are important to proper adornment, but they are also social acts because they require the assistance of another person. This kind of cooperative effort is common in many communities around the world. Adolescents use arm and leg bands made of bark fibre that they wrap around limbs to emphasize muscles and to enhance their attractiveness. Men wrap wide bark strips around their ankles to guard against thorns and snake bites. White belts designate youth, but men with children use color. Red and yellow feather earrings are symbolically important as an integral part of life cycle ceremonies and the initiation of tribal chiefs. Headdresses symbolize wealth. The men cover their bodies with *urucu*, a red pigment widely used in the Amazon. It indicates the wearer's willingness to interact with others and makes him sexually attractive to women (p. 158). If he is angry or in ritual seclusion, he won't apply urucu to his body.

For the Mehinaku, women's dress is less complex than that of men, perhaps because the men are on public display in the more visible places of the village. Women's basic dress is a simple "beige-colored" twine wrapped around the hips a number of times. "The width of the belt is a rough indicator of a woman's age, ritual status, and personal mood. If she is sad, ashamed, or in mourning for a husband or lover, she removes strands from her belt" (Gregor 1977:162). As the woman goes through life, the belt gets thinner. Another single stranded belt holds a small piece of bark that hides the pubis. A cord attached to the bottom runs through the labia of the vagina, and through the buttocks, coming out in back somewhat like a tail. The garment is intended to make her beautiful, and the men consider it sexy. Like the men, women wear ligatures especially around the calf to make it appear larger. These and other adornments tell of the woman's age, mood, wealth, and sexual accessibility.

From the conservative body concealment of the Pilgrims, to the loose, revealing look of the 1920s' flappers, to the braless, mini-skirted fashion of the 1970s, feminine dress in the United States paralleled changes in the larger socioeconomic context and accompanied transformations in conceptions of gender and sexuality. In general, the changes in feminine dress signified a new freedom and recognition of sexuality. Men's attire changed too, but less dramatically. Contrary to the Mehinaku, today's clothing styles in the United States tend to blur distinctions among gender, class, age, and authority. As a consequence it is more difficult in many cases to read clothing for these social indicators. Clothing styles in the United States are ever changing because they are driven by the fashion industry, whose advertisements are often rife with sexual messages, particularly with respect to women's bodies. Advertisements contain messages about the inner-self and group identity and are directed particularly at the young who control a large amount of disposable income.

Sex, Desire, and Modern Primitives

We noted earlier that Westerners frequently have used their often flawed understandings of other cultures for their own purposes. This appropriation of the Other characterizes the tattooing, scarification, and piercing movement known as the "modern primitives." This movement has its origins in the hippie era of the 1960s, but emerged in the 1980s in San Francisco among alternative communities, for example, gay and lesbian, S/M, and New Age (Rosenblatt 1997:301). In the 1960s, tattoo artists became fascinated with full-body Japanese tattooing. Until then, tattooing had been associated with bikers, sailors, carnival sideshows, and working-class men. Today, tattooing and other forms of body modification, while not exactly mainstream, are much more widely in evidence and generally provoke little comment in their moderate use. In their desire to make personal statements, the modern primitives differ from the original tattoo recipients. The current generation does not select predesigned patterns from the display wall, known as "flash," but fashion new designs with more personal meaning. This section draws from Rosenblatt's (1997) seminal article that explores how body modifications and sexuality of the Other have inspired modern primitives.

Modern primitives look to other cultures as sources of inspiration and authenticity as they resist the pressures of mainstream North American culture. They are particularly drawn to Japan, Samoa, Borneo, and other cultures of the Pacific where body modification is mainstream. They rely on the "ethnographic authority" of anthropological accounts of such practices (Rosenblatt 1997:299). Modern primitives see body modification and ritual as a basic, and therefore authentic, human need that counters a capitalistic society concerned with pushing the desire for consumer goods. Another source of inspiration is what they take to be primitive sexual desire that predates the desire for goods. "The association of the primitive with sexuality seems to be a constant—modern primitives in the United States today valorize a primitive that, like its predecessor, is more open about sexual desire and less concerned with consumer goods" (p. 296). The new primitives form a resistance group against the press of modern life and thus join a particular moment in history with ideas about sex, "selves, society, and experiences" (p. 288).

Just how is it, Rosenblatt asks, that tattoos, scarification, and piercing come to incorporate knowledge of other cultures and to reclaim the body seized by mainstream culture (p. 290)? Those selves who modify their bodies construct meaning from these markings as they are used in other cultures; they imagine "resemblances" between what they do in modern culture and the ancient ways of the Other. The connection is further anchored in the visible marks made on the skin. What they and the Other do are parallel acts cognitively connected by the new primitives. Rosenblatt recounts one story of a person who got the idea for piercing from seeing photographs in *National Geographic* of tribesmen in Papua New Guinea exhibiting nose rings (p. 311). He thought this was an authentic expression of the precapitalist self. But tattooing involves more than just connecting with primitives. "Tattooing is both a public and a private act. When people talk about their tattoos, about getting tattoos, and living with tattoos, they move back and forth between what it means to them and the reactions other people have to their being tattooed" (p. 306).

Modern primitives derive great power from the emotional (recovering some of your inner-self) and ritual (a formal transformation) elements in their modification experiences. "The permanence of a tattoo, and its perceived connection to some inner self, lend a kind of authenticity to tattooing and give people a sense that in getting a tattoo they have done something real about their relationship to the world" (p. 309). These "social inscriptions" on the skin can, as Mary Douglas saw, clearly mark the skin as a contested area between the self and the public. For example, the idea that with tattooing and other body modification one reclaims the body and makes a real change in one's relationships is attractive to some women who have been told at one time that they are not supposed to have sexual pleasure and at another time that they are simply sexual objects.

Although tattoos are often considered beautiful and erotic by new primitives, piercing and scarification convey even more erotic content. Multiple ear piercing, and nose, eyebrow, mouth, lip, tongue and navel piercing are especially evident in urban places and on college campuses. What is not so visible is the nipple and genital piercing that is more closely related to erotics than aesthetics and probably not confined just to those who could be labeled new primitives. Nipple and genital piercing are usually done to intensify sexual experience and sometimes for the pleasure of being pierced.

For all of their opposition to modern North American culture, most modern primitives are seeking ways to feel good about or "improve" themselves and thus may be engaging in practices that are essentially no different than mainstream techniques, such as assertiveness training or the use of self-improvement books. Rosenblatt says that the "popularity of tattoos has paralleled a general cultural preoccupation with the body that has led to a widespread obsession with diet, and plastic surgery" (1997:310). North American women (and increasingly men) today often undergo forms of body modification such as face lifts, liposuction, and breast augmentation to conform to current, popular images of physical beauty.

Male and Female Genital Cutting

Virtually all cultures find it important to mark the passage of individuals through important life stages. Known collectively as *rites of passage* (Van Gennep 1960), these rituals are another form of embodiment. Although the number of stages that are celebrated varies across cultures, the most important and common ones are usually those marking birth, puberty, marriage, and death. These are considered critical transitions in an individual's life span because each stage signals a change in social status and relationships, with new obligations, new possibilities, and new dangers. Marriage, for example, establishes a relationship between two groups of people that in many places in the world is more of an economic and political contract than a union of two individuals on the basis of personal chemistry. The public celebration of marriage establishes its legitimacy and prepares the way for the legitimacy of any offspring born of a marriage. When marriage and living arrangements are private and ambiguous, public questions of its legitimacy may be raised. Especially where groups rather than individuals are concerned, such uncertainties can lead to tension and conflict over rights to offspring and other matters of inheritance. If such observances, on the other hand, are conducted properly in the public arena, they reduce ambiguity and make events flow more smoothly. Rites of passage serve to coordinate critical points in the life span of individuals with group goals and assist in creating a competent, legitimate, and moral adult.

A subset of rites of passage known as adult initiation rites is most closely connected with sexuality because it marks sexual and social maturity. Females' rites are the most common, but because they are less public and dramatic than male rites they are not well described in the ethnographic literature. During these rituals, men and women may receive any number and types of marks on their bodies, have their heads shaved, or have their teeth removed. Some rites require genital operations. Male initiation rites often include incisions in the penis.[1] These procedures are potentially dangerous because of possible hemorrhaging and infection. Cuts are made with a variety of instruments, none sterile. *Circumcision*, the complete removal of the foreskin of the penis, is an operation conducted widely in different geographical locations, including the United States. Health authorities in the United States have in fact vacillated about whether to recommend circumcision soon after birth as a health measure (for the prevention of penile cancer and reduction in the incidence of urinary track infection). Yet, in the United States 90 percent of Jewish male infants are circumcised, as are 81 percent of non-Hispanic whites, about 50 percent of African Americans, and just under 40 percent Hispanic American men (Lauman et al. 1997). *Superincision* involves cutting only the foreskin lengthwise, a practice commonly found in some Polynesian groups. *Subincision* is the opening of the bottom of the penis along virtually its entire length, requiring men as a result to squat when they urinate. The incision is not allowed to heal, but is kept open. This practice occurs almost exclusively in Australia (Gregersen 1996:108).

Why these painful rituals? It may be that in many cases boys must be toughened for fighting with neighboring groups. A clear identity as a tough warrior has adaptive value in a culture where male dominance and constant warfare are the norm. Most explanations of male initiation rites center on the separation of a boy from his mother, her influence (see Gilmore 1990), and the domestic domain in which he spends his early years, and on the related difficulty of acquiring an appropriate manhood. At puberty, the boy is removed from his house to the men's house, or to the intermediate boys' house, where he undergoes training, fasting, or any number of ordeals as part of the process of becoming a man. It is also a time of instruction in important cultural and religious matters known by adult males.

Transformed from local custom to global issue, few cultural practices have so galvanized international debate as another form of embodiment, female genital cutting. "The issue strikes numerous nerves, as it challenges fundamental understandings of body, self, sexuality, family, and morality, and it plays upon tensions relating to cultural difference, the relationship between women and 'tradition,' and the legacy of colonial-era depictions of gender relations in non-Western countries" (Walley 1997:406).

The debate is usually cast in stark, opposing "terms of *either* cultural relativism or politically informed outrage" (p. 406), which oversimplify its real complexity. These operations are quite painful (some activists call them torture), can be a threat to health, and easily provoke, in Western minds, moral indignation and demands for their immediate cessation. The public in Europe and the United States became aware of genital operations during the 1990s in a series of highly publicized trials, as immigrants from the Sudan and sub-Saharan Africa attempted to import the practice and ran afoul of various local laws. These incidents were immediately elevated to international debates by human rights and feminist organizations and international health agencies. The issue is not as simple as it seems, and involves a number of deficiencies.

The first problem with these debates is that they commonly use ambiguous and prejudicial language. Although female genital operations are commonly referred to as *female circumcision* or *female genital mutilation* (FGM) as if all practices are the same, Christine Walley

(1997:429) notes that they really do not exist as a category because the label covers such a wide variety of practices, which occur in different cultural contexts and have somewhat different meanings. Female circumcision derives its name from the fact that the clitoris, thought in some cultures to be analogous to the penis, is excised. Partially or completely removing the clitoris is, in medical terminology, *clitoridectomy*. Usually, this operation is accompanied by a complete or partial removal of the labia minora and sometimes portions of the labia majora as well. Both FGM and female circumcision are, however, controversial labels. "Mutilation" suggests torture, but circumcision, provoking moral outrage, something more benign, is seen more in the light of relativistic tolerance (Walley 1997:408). Another practice often associated with these cuttings is *infibulation,* a practice where the inner surfaces of the labia are made raw and then sewn together or fixed with thorns or the woman's legs are tied together for 40 days, during which period healing seals the vagina. A small stick is inserted when the vagina is closed in order to leave a small opening as it heals through which pass urine and menstrual blood. The vagina is opened upon marriage for conception to take place. In some cultures, a woman may be resealed after giving birth. Some women believe that because a woman's vagina is tighter for several months following reopening, she gives greater sexual pleasure to her husband (Gruenbaum 2001).

The extent of these practices varies from culture to culture, but all are excruciatingly painful and are performed typically with various sharp instruments under unsanitary conditions with no anesthesia. The pain, however, is something that recipients of these operations are usually prepared for. Walley observed a dual circumcision ceremony for both boys and girls in Kikhome, located in a western province of Kenya, near the Ugandan border:

> The boys were cut by a male circumcisor while standing; the girls were excised by a woman as they sat with legs spread on the ground, their backs supported by their sponsors. The crucial test was for the initiate to show no pain, to neither change expression nor even blink, during the cutting. Remarkably enough to my friend and I, the initiates remained utterly stoic, and expressionless throughout. We were told it is this ability to withstand the ordeal that confers adulthood, that allows one to marry and have children, and that binds one to one's age mates. (Walley 1997:410)

While cultures may prepare initiates for the pain they will feel, these operations do carry health risks. Infibulation particularly carries a high risk of incurring chronic health problems from scar tissue, repeated infections, hemorrhage, urine retention, abscess, gangrene, and damage to adjacent organs. Scar tissue may make penetration quite painful, and the reduction of the clitoris would make sexual pleasure even more difficult to achieve, although little solid information is available on the sexual pleasure of infibulated women (Walley 1997:415). One survey done in the Sudan and reported by Daniel Gordon (1991) indicated that 75 percent of women had never experienced sexual pleasure or were uninterested in it. Walley (1997:415) cites investigators who suspect that orgasms may be achieved through other means, for example, by fantasizing or by manipulating other sensory areas.

Female genital operations (including both clitoridectomy and infibulation) occur in rural populations that are largely under Islamic influence and are concentrated across central Africa and the horn of Africa (northeastern section) (Rahman and Toubia 2001). The practices are always found in conjunction with male circumcision, with the two usually seen locally as balancing each other. Most Islamic cultures, however, do not include these practices, and Islamic scholars say that there is no religious justification for them, although most groups who practice genital operations believe that there is because they preserve virginity, improve hygiene, purify the body, control excess sex (women are assumed to be naturally oversexed), and promote fertility.

Most populations practice clitoridectomy and infibulation as a rite of puberty, but Gordon (1991) reports that in Egypt and the Sudan, the operations take place well before puberty and usher girls into a state of "social puberty," with further restrictions placed on them (see also Gruenbaum 2001). In the Sudan, over 98 percent of 3,210 women surveyed had received clitoridectomy, and 83 percent had been infibulated. Ninety percent of the operations were performed by midwives, or *dayas*. Procedures in Egypt appear to be more moderate and experienced by less than half of the women. Both governments now ban the more severe operations, which they regard as a health risk. In Somalia, almost all girls received some form of genital incision, and about 80 percent are infibulated. In Kenya, about 50 percent of the females undergo genital modification.

The women who experience these practices live in a system where virginity and family honor are fundamentally linked with each other. A man living under this system will, traditionally, not marry an uninfibulated woman because to do so would dishonor his family. Women who are not infibulated are by definition not virgins regardless of their actual sexual experience. The ultimate goal of this practice is probably found in male efforts to control the reproductive resources of women, and Gordon (1991) takes as one indication of this function the case that women are often reinfibulated after giving birth so that male control continues. Moreover, in Egypt and Sudan, initiation rituals are performed well in advance of puberty, while menopausal women are released from traditional constraints on their activities. The utilitarian motive to control reproductive potential should not lead us to take less seriously the degree to which both men and women have internalized their culture's norms and values and commit emotionally to them.

The justifications for female genital operations are learned and therefore can be unlearned; cultures change and often come to look at some traditional practices as unwise and harmful, or simply outdated. Indeed, many of the countries involved in these practices have passed laws against at least their more severe forms, although the laws are unevenly enforced and generally can be enforced only if there is a complaint, which is unlikely in remote rural locations. In recent years, both international and local activists have demonstrated against female circumcision. Some authorities suggest, at a minimum, that the operations should be conducted in hospitals under sterile conditions with anesthesia. Others suggest less painful and health threatening substitution rites. Young men in some areas are becoming less insistent that their future wife be infibulated.

Proposed changes will have a better chance of success if they are not piecemeal fixes, but tuned to the wider cultural system of which the operations are a part (Gruenbaum 2001). It is not just genital cutting alone that is important, but how specific types of people are involved in the practice. For example, the basic social identity and status of a woman is in many communities presently bound inextricably to genital operations. Should genital operations suddenly be eliminated, on what grounds will a woman claim her identity and her value for marriage? Her place in society? If proof of virginity plays a key role in a pattern of marriage choice, bride wealth, and lineage continuity, what happens to this pattern if the cornerstone is removed? Is family honor transferable to another practice? Midwives who conduct these operations as well as deinfibulating women at marriage earn prestige and wealth by virtue of their expertise. Would they actively resist change? How is wealth then generated in these poor populations?

Walley (1997) cites a number of issues that have emerged as a result of the debate about female genital operations. First, there is the question of properly labeling disparate kinds of genital operations. The power to name is often the power to control; changing the name is a political act, which is fundamentally conflicting. When powerful outsiders use the term *mutilation*, they take a moral stance that can lead to heavy-handed tactics to abolish the practice regardless of local wishes. National and international health authorities are such powerful outsiders, among others.

A second problem is discerning the voices of the African women themselves. In the Kenyan village of Kikhome, Walley did not gain the impression that women necessarily agreed with each other on clitoridectomy; they were, in fact, ambivalent themselves. Their "voices" changed with shifting social contexts (p. 412). Nevertheless, African women who do not necessarily support female operations may resist efforts by outside feminist groups to co-opt the issue. This reaction recalls the specter of colonial relationships and the power differential behind the efforts to impose Western standards on Africans. Walley points out also that there is a tendency for the outside "to characterize African women as thoroughly oppressed victims of patriarchy, ignorance, or both, not as social actors in their own right" (p. 419), when, in fact, African women themselves have initiated grassroots movements in opposition to current cutting practices.

A third problem is what Walley (p. 425–27) calls a "hardening of tradition." By this she means the tendency of outsiders to see these practices as part of an unchanging, primitive culture in contrast to the modernizing, rational cultures of the West, thereby overlooking the changes that actually are taking place. Finally, she notes that feminists who call for change often find themselves uncomfortably aligned with the media and their neocolonial attitudes. The international debate about female operations constantly borders on racism by invoking images of the African primitive and his/her unchanging ways. In an attempt to head off such a view, anthropologists, including feminist anthropologists, might take a cultural relativist stance that valorizes local cultures, but in doing so also might undercut the efforts of local women to eliminate, or modify, the practice of female genital operations.

The questions posed previously are not intended as an apology for genital operations or as an advocacy for their continuation. In fact, changes in laws and attitudes toward genital operations are occurring in the countries where they are practiced, and have been for some time. Instead, the questions are consistent with the principles of analysis and understanding emphasized in the first chapter and are intended as corrective measures against the study of sexuality in isolation of its cultural context. These same principles inform efforts to change cultural practices. Applied programs are more effective if they are driven by a cultural understanding that is attuned to how local customs fit into their cultural context, not by isolated medical remedies or moral doctrines. Local populations are often quite sensitive to calls for change that come from outsiders and see such as an example of "cultural imperialism." Further, this international debate over local custom reminds us that there is a "growing impermeability of national boundaries" (Walley 1997:406) in the globalization process.

Blood Magic

Blood magic is about the symbolic potency of menstrual blood, about a substance that flows from the body and therefore must be explained and given meaning (Douglas 1966). But the symbolic approach has limitations, some of which are indicated below (Buckley and Gottlieb 1988). *Menstrual taboos* are widespread, sharing similar characteristics cross-culturally but also featuring some local differences in detail. Generally, menstruating women are seen as dangerous and offensive, and their movements and activities therefore must be controlled by certain prohibitions and magical safeguards. Suzanne Frayser (1985:221) finds that 70 percent of 30 societies believe that menstrual flow is dangerous to others. Orthodox Jews, some Christian sects, and Islamic groups place restrictions on the activities and movements of menstruating women.[2] Women may be prohibited from interacting with men, serving men food, or having sex with their husband. It may be that only the blood is considered dangerous or that in addition, the woman herself is dangerous. There is no single taboo that holds cross-culturally, but rather there exists a wide variety of rules of conduct with somewhat different purposes and meanings. The prohibitions attached to menstruation may be severe, moderate, or mild. Frayser (1985:223) reports that 31 percent (of 38 societies) have severe restrictions, citing, for example, the Gond of India where menstruating women are placed in seclusion in a hut isolated from other huts and with a door facing away from the village. All food is cooked by others in a separate pot and placed outside the door. Men cannot come anywhere near the hut. Crocker and Crocker (1994:34) report for the Canela that "after their first menstruation, girls underwent similar dietary restrictions. . . ."

The meanings or the prohibitions of menstrual taboos, however, are not imbued with a positive or negative value. The word taboo is Polynesian and means "to mark thoroughly" (Buckley and Gottlieb 1988). As such it has more to do with holy/forbidden than positive/negative. It does not necessarily mean oppression, and it can restrict men as much as women. The common practice of secluding menstruating women in a separate hut can function to increase solidarity among women.

What explanations are offered for these blood taboos? Thomas Buckley and Alma Gottlieb (1988) review a number of explanations. One explanation is that men invented them to oppress women. In fact we do not know who invented the practice; it could just as well have been invented by women themselves. It does not necessarily oppress them anyway. This explanation is too simplistic and casts women as victims, even though men are controlled at these times as well. Second, Freudian psychology interprets such taboos as a neurosis and related to castration anxiety in men. Again, this explanation is too simplistic and based on questionable links between individual psychology and culture. Another explanation follows Mary Douglas's line of thought about purity and danger and suggests that menstrual blood is a form of pollution. Because menstrual blood leaves the body, it is out of its natural place and is thus dangerous to symbolic order. Against the pollution idea is the fact that some cultures see menstrual blood not as a threat but as life-affirming and a cause for joyful celebration.

The Ashanti of West Africa have powerful menstrual taboos but also celebrate menarche, giving girls gifts and congratulations as they watch dances performed and songs sung in their honor.

Other cultures, because they believe conception occurs with the mingling of blood and semen, see menstruation as a lost opportunity for fertilization. In one culture, placing a drop of menstrual blood in a man's food kills him, while in another it causes him to fall in love. Moreover, in some cultures, only some men are vulnerable to the potency of menstrual blood, usually husbands. In the past, anthropological understanding of this topic has been dominated by males, but female scholars are now turning their attention to the perceptions and experiences of the women who are subjected to these taboos (Buckley and Gottlieb 1988).

THE BIOLOGICAL BASIS OF
LOVE AND ATTRACTION

Male display, female choice, pair bonding, and continuing sexual receptivity are important elements of sexual reproduction in many species. They are key concepts in sociobiology and evolutionary psychology, which emphasize the genetics behind behavior. Just how and to what extent these elements govern our sexuality and shape our experiences of romantic passion remains a topic of debate. While the theoretical stance that credits biology for our behavior is controversial, we need to leave open the dialogue between the biological and cultural proponents to be consistent with our interactive model. As sexually reproducing creatures, mating and parenting are critical to us. Because human females do not have a defined period of estrus, a prolonged period of intense attraction between mates might insure a truly committed effort on the part of the male to produce offspring with only one female, rather than trying to mate with a number of females. The same prolonged period of attraction and attachment also serves the male protecting and provisioning functions that enhance the survival of mother and offspring. Romantic passion thus may very well be an important feature of our evolutionary adaptation. On the other hand, it is also true that relatives of the mother can protect and provision her and her offspring in the absence of a committed father.

Helen Fisher (1992:24) observes that attraction and attachment are two basic components of romantic love, that they are "primary, panhuman emotions much like fear, anger, joy, sadness, and surprise, that these feelings are based in brain chemistry, as are the other primary emotions, [and] that human romantic love stems from mammalian biochemical systems of affiliation" which evolved millions of years ago in conjunction with our reproductive strategy—*serial pair bonding*. Serial bonding refers to multiple mates over time, but only one at any given time. Fisher points out that basing attraction and attachment in evolved biochemical systems does not mean that we are inevitably compelled by them to act in a particular fashion. Culture also plays an important role in shaping our biochemical responses. Attachment can be seen as an "emergent system" that develops from a "variety of physiological, sociocultural, and experiential factors" along different paths in different cultures (Hinton 1999:312).

An initial state of attraction and infatuation triggers in the brain a cascade of chemicals that are cousins to amphetamines. On the other hand, in the presence of a long-term partner, the brain releases endorphins which are soothing (a natural pain killer). The loss of a partner in the latter case leaves one without endorphins' calming effect. The early excitement of love and its chemical releases causes some individuals to become "attraction junkies" who crave the initial thrill of falling in love and triggering a chemical cascade. In these cases, the attachment phase may be limited to three to four years for both the male and the female, after which the male mates with another female. Fisher accumulated cross-cultural evidence that strongly suggests that divorces generally peak at around four years in many different cultures, although the period may well be less lengthy. In her view, attachment and attraction are generally followed by a phase of *detachment*. While our "neuroanatomy and neurochemical" makeup are responsible for these "affiliative emotions," we are not necessarily condemned to an endless cycle of detaching from mates and seeking new attachments. Other data indicate that having repeated offspring and aging together builds a companionate relationship that produces other pleasant morphine-like chemicals. Rather than constraining us to one kind of pair-bonding, Fisher observes that we are provided with the flexibility to respond to specific cultural settings with variations in mating patterns (see also Hinton 1997:312). For example, protecting and provisioning functions can be assumed by relatives rather than by a male lovers or by another male.

In a series of works, R. Bowlby (1969) and M. D. Ainsworth (1964) suggest that future social relationships are constructed on the basis of infant attachment, or bonding, with caretakers, typically but not necessarily a mother. The child can bond with more than one person. Positive bonding, or *secure attachment*, sets up the expectation that future relationships will also be positive. If bonding does not occur, then future relationships may be difficult to form and to sustain. Insecure attachment results in shorter (and perhaps more intense) love relationships as well as negative emotions. From a developmental perspective, our human capacity to affiliate with others must be positively reinforced by early experience that serves as a template for future relationships.

Our hormonal system is also involved in attachment and infatuation. Pheremones are chemical odors that enhance bonding between child and parent, and possibly attracts lovers. It also regulates ovulation. Oxytocin is a pituitary hormone that stimulates labor contractions and facilitates the flow of breast milk.

BEAUTY AND DESIRE

Mangaian (Cook Islands, Central Pacific) women often are considered erotic if they have a wide pelvis and large hips, perhaps because these features are thought to indicate greater fertility. It is a common value that men should have a large penis (it is not always clear whether both genders agree on this). Mangaian men talk much about female genitalia, especially the shape and size of the mons veneris; some appreciate a fat vulva or long clitoris (Marshall 1971).

The Taita men of Kenya (East Africa) like women with bright eyes, a pretty, broad nose, and a full mouth with thick lips (Bell 1995:196). Women should have a wide smile with white teeth, soft skin, "delicate" eyes, high cheekbones, and small ears set close to the head. Female body shapes should be heavy with large breasts (for nourishing infants), thick legs, and small ankles. Buttocks should be firm, and women should walk as if floating. For great beauty, women should have a pleasing personality. Women profess to like men who are intelligent and good providers. They should have a strong face with no hair (considered ugly when on the face). They should have shining eyes and a thick neck to carry the head proudly. They should be well-muscled and have copper brown to reddish brown skin. Their penis should be neither too large nor too small. Neither men nor women really expect to marry their ideals, but they enjoy speculating about the possibility. These descriptions value different qualities in a mate. Men emphasize the physical characteristics of women, and women care more about the personality and social standing of men (p. 197). This distinction is common elsewhere in the world, including the United States. Evolutionary psychologists would suggest the evolutionary importance of men focusing on women's reproductive health, and women on characteristics necessary for providing and protecting.

All cultures impose on the human form ideals of beauty and desirability. Our physical desire is triggered largely by our reaction to physical attractiveness, although other personal characteristics and erotic settings are often involved too. Our ideal of physical attractiveness is governed by our cultural standards. While cultural standards vary from culture to culture, and even within a particular culture, there may be a few universal characteristics of beauty and desirability, especially signs of what is considered good *health*. But even in this category, cultural standards intrude. For example, a large body can be considered healthy and attractive in one culture and unhealthy and ugly in another. As Edgar Gregersen (1994:96) points out, the ideal of *cleanliness* has changed throughout history in the Western world, often in association with changing religious ideas. There was a time from early Christianity to the 1400s when cleanliness was *not* next to godliness. Attitudes began to change with the opening of public baths. If cleanliness is not universal, it is nevertheless a very common value. *Body symmetry* may be another universal, and *age* still another. Donald Buss (1994) has suggested that men desire young and attractive women because they signal reproductive success. However, men may be predisposed to prefer young women, but this is not a determinative influence on their choice of a mate.

In writing his 1929 classic, Malinowski took an interesting approach to the subject of erotic desire. He began with what was considered ugly—advanced age and disease. What is ugly to the Trobriand Islanders is opposite to beauty ([1929]1987:243). However, a negative appearance does not actually prevent people from having sexual contact and having children, perhaps because the favored sexual position does not require a body length embrace. What is considered beautiful? "Vigour, vitality, and strength, a well proportioned body, a smooth and properly pigmented, but not too dark skin are the basis of physical beauty for the native" (pp. 248–49). It is common to value women's breasts—firm and well developed, and men's build and size—tall and narrow. However, the focus of attention is on the face in many respects.

The face is painted in various ways with red, black, and white pigment to accentuate features according to cultural values. Trobrianders find eyes to be of particular erotic interest and biting off eye lashes during sexual activity is common. Eyes should be shining and small. Lips should be full and well defined, but not protruding. The nose should be neither too flat nor too sharp. Ears should be neither too large nor too small and should not stand out from the head. The lobe of the ear must be pierced and decorated with an earring. Blackened teeth (by placing a mangrove root against the teeth at night) is considered beautiful, but most Trobrianders, in fact, do not blacken their teeth.

Body hair is considered ugly, and the body therefore should be kept shaven. Trobrianders bathe frequently and are quite sensitive to body dirt and odors. They often practice a beauty magic (mentioned at the beginning of the chapter) which is not directly related to sex but to making men more pleasing in general and, in certain ritual contexts, fit to be rewarded with gifts. They recognize that physical characteristics of beauty may not, however, be sufficient for either gender in marriage, where other qualities of character and personality come into play as being important.

In the United States, the media parade ideal male and female body images in front of viewers constantly. Men want to bulk up and women to slim down. These ideals can lead to eating disorders among women (and increasingly among men), such as the potentially fatal *anorexia nervosa* (a severe restriction of food intake), and to steroid abuse (especially for men who want to bulk up). To a significant segment of the population, the ideal of personal attractiveness is joined with having a healthy body.

Studies of college students and body image (Rathus, Nevid, and Fichner-Rathus 2000:190–91) indicate that undergraduate women prefer to date men who are about six inches taller than they, and men prefer women who are about four and half inches shorter. Tall women are not so desirable, but neither are short women. Men prefer slender women, but not as slender as women think, and men misperceive how lean women want them to be. Women see themselves as heavier than the ideal. Men focus more on physical attributes of women, especially if sexuality alone is of concern, than women do on men. None of these studies exclude the importance of other social and personal qualities such as good humor, industriousness, and companionship.

Body images are not just abstract conceptions, but schema that have real consequences for all of us. Bodies are inhabited by culturally and personally formed selves. In the contemporary United States, body image and self-image often seem essentially inseparable, and neither can be disconnected from sexuality. Cultural ideas of sexuality, body image, and self-image converge on the self. The components are interactive with one another, working on two levels: our public presentations of ourselves and our private thoughts and feelings. The adaptive self struggles to adjust to these various and often conflicting forces.

ROMANTIC PASSION

All humans have the capacity to become intensely and sexually attracted to another person, but Westerners have not always been prepared to find such sentiments in other cultures. This bias arose out of a period of time in Western history when love was seen as an idealistic, but ineluctable emotion that could be understood and experienced only as a matter of cultural refinement. In short, love was seen as a cultivated property of civilization, especially upper classes. Because non-

Westerners were not civilized, they could not know love. In fact, Western bias often took the more strident view that uncivilized, heathen savages were closer to animals and therefore regularly fell prey to their "baser instincts" and lived in a state of sexual promiscuity. That primitives could love was not a question seriously entertained. Further, love was associated in the West with the rise of individualism, which was foreign, the argument went, to other cultures where individuals acceded to the demands of the group. In the latter case, the economic and political goals of the group were the only legitimate reasons for marriage. There would, then, be no reason for group-oriented cultures to place high value on individual emotional states as an acceptable motive for marriage. Excluding love as a sufficient reason for marriage, however, does not mean that it does not exist. Romantic passion, love, is always a possibility in human populations regardless of ideals and institutions that favor mating or marriage for other reasons.

The European ideal of romantic love was a product of a historical period of time, a time of courtly love, in the eleventh and twelfth centuries and supported subsequently by the growing importance of individual relationships, especially in marriage. This ideal of courtly love (troubadours, knights, chivalry) downplayed the sexual realization of love, although in practice this was not always the case. Indeed, feelings of love were thought to be intensified by love unreturned, and without sexual involvement. This slant on love is at least as old as Plato, who felt that true love excludes the physical component (Bullough 1976:164–65). Platonic love is spiritual, intellectual love without sex.

In various periods of Western history, and with various social classes and groups, sex as a component of love was recognized or ignored to varying degrees. The body was often either a vessel for higher spiritual and intellectual achievements, or fundamentally lustful and sinful, or both at the same time. The role of lust, simple but intense sexual attraction and satisfaction, seemed frequently to be linked to a view of the body as something to be controlled by the civilized mind. The Europeans often saw other cultures as sexually immoral, lustful, unable to control the base impulses of their bodies. Sexual "depravities" were among the first customs they tried to control in their colonies. To civilize native peoples was to enable them to control their bodies in ways acceptable to Westerners. At the same time, the idealization of love in Europe masked to a degree the actual frequency of premarital and extramarital sexual behavior that likely occurred there.

Until the late 1700s, North Americans saw sex as appropriate only for reproduction in the context of marriage and family. In the latter part of the century our focus began to change as the courting phase turned to matters of sexuality and intimacy. "Open expressions of sentiment replaced the religious language of earlier couples" (D'Emilio and Freedman 1997). Whereas earlier, affection had been assumed to grow out of marriage, now it was an assumed precondition to engagement. By the late 1800s to the early 1900s, the theme of love and sex had become entrenched in North American culture. These sentiments surfaced in the frank discussions (for the times) of sexuality that "appeared in the diaries and letters of engaged couples" (p. 76). Indeed, these explicit expressions heightened erotic desires. Women were no doubt relieved to share a reduced emphasis on their reproductive function—many felt worn down by frequent pregnancies and a high infant mortality rate—and inspired by the increasing importance of intimacy and love. Moreover, the trend introduced a new note of personal choice of a mate, which must have been welcome as well (p. 84).

William Jankowiak (1995:4) defines romantic passion: "Presently, romantic passion (or romantic love or infatuation) is defined as any intense attraction involving the idealization of the other within an erotic context. The idealization carries with it the desire for intimacy and the pleasurable expectation of enduring for some time into the future." He notes that three elements characterize romantic passion, *idealization, intensity*, and *eroticism*. Love implies intimacy, and a sharing of experiences as well. In the West, we qualify love by speaking of its different forms; mother love, parental love, romantic love, brotherly love, patriotic love, and more, without the erotic component except in romantic love. We are most interested here in romantic passion as defined by Jankowiak.

The subject of love has been embraced by countless poets, novelists, composers, philosophers, and playwrights over the centuries. Modern mass media dwell on it endlessly. In spite of the popularity of the topic, however, love has held little research interest for scientists until recent decades, and few solid studies of romantic passion in non-Western cultures currently exist (Jankowiak 1995:1). Now a variety of disciplines have devoted research to the phenomenon of love, and as a result of recent inquiries, we are beginning to understand it better.

In 1979, Dorothy Tennov produced a cross-cultural study of love, or *limerance*, based on over 500 case studies. She was able to reduce the common elements of limerance to thirteen. As Harris (1995:101) observes, Tennov's work made it easier to work on the subject cross-culturally without the usual linguistic, cultural, and definitional problems of love. However, Harris sees Tennov's scheme as being too rigid and devised her own, although it is based on Tennov's. Here is an abbreviated version of Harris's list.

1. *Desire for union* or merger, both physical and emotional (initially sexual).

2. *Idealization* of the beloved (called crystallization by Tennov) that maximizes the love object's positive qualities and mini-

mizes negative qualities.

3. *Exclusivity* is a focus of emotion and desire on one particular person and a desire for this exclusive focus to be returned.

4. *Intrusive thinking* about the love object is a cognitive preoccupation with the love object that interferes with other cognitive tasks.

5. *Emotional dependency* is an emotional state dependent on reciprocation and especially on the maintenance of physical and emotional access to the beloved.

6. *A reordering of motivational hierarchies* or life priorities where central importance is accorded the maintenance of the relationship.

7. *A powerful sense of empathy and concern* for the beloved (based more on self-interest than altruism). (pp. 102–3)

Harris employed this reduced scheme in her restudy of Mangaians (the same Pacific Island culture studied by Marshall) and found it to be effective. She concluded that compared to North American patterns of love, the Mangaians differ only in emphasis (1995:23). The general difference is that the Mangaians are much more comfortable with, and expressive of, sexual matters than we are in North America. These emphases, however, can be important as they reflect specific ways in which love (as well as other emotions) are developed in different cultures.

SUMMARY

We make practical and symbolic use of the body. We develop attitudes and values about it and its functions, and we use its physical presence to help us to think about more abstract matters such as society, purity, and danger. Wrapping the body in cultural meaning is embodiment. We embody with clothing, painting, incisions, and menstrual prohibitions for a variety of cultural reasons. One of the most dramatic forms of embodiment is seen in male circumcision rites that mark the passage of boys into manhood. Although male rites are less common than female rites, they are more public and have been given more attention. Recently, however, female circumcision rites have taken center stage and become a matter of international debate. Because they are associated with fundamental female identity and status, and fully integrated into the local marriage and kinship system, they may be somewhat difficult to change. Another form of embodiment is found in taboos associated with menstrual flow. Most commonly, these taboos isolate women from men, particularly from their husbands, for the duration of the flow. While much is made by outsiders of the negative aspects of blood taboos, menstrual flow often leads to celebrations of fertility and may work in some cases to increase female solidarity.

Ideas about beauty, health, and fertility, which may be partly influenced by evolutionary processes and partly influenced by culture, shape our mating choices. These body images in North America are commercially manipulated and associated with other images of fun and personal worth. Romantic passion is a capacity present in all human groups, but often not traditionally accepted as a legitimate and compelling reason for marriage. In the West and in the United States in particular, it is given as the principal reason for marriage. Cross-cultural studies indicate that romantic passion subsides after three or four years (as reflected in the rise of divorce rates at this time). At the same time, other pleasant biochemical processes have been found to support long-term relationships.

CRITICAL INQUIRY

1. Does the United States have initiation rites of any kind? If not, should it? Why? Can you design one that might work? Should it in any way be connected with sexuality?

2. What other forms of embodiment can you think of that are not discussed in the text?

3. Do you think it is cultural imperialism to pressure those cultures practicing female circumcision to change their ways, or do you see it as a matter of basic human rights?

NOTES

[1] Some male initiation rites do not necessarily include incisions but instead the honor of wearing an article of clothing such as a belt or of being adorned with a certain painted pattern.

[2] The West in general holds a negative view of menstruation.

Chapter Four

Sex Patterns

All of you boys look at this elder. What do you think he has done? Heard the law this moment and grown to be so big? All of them [the men] "sucked" the penis . . . and grew big. All of them can inseminate you; all of you can suck penises. If you suck them, you will grow bigger quickly. (Herdt 1987:149)

A man picks a woman he is not related to and walks out to her. He swiftly completes the sex act and stands up. Then the next man, seeing the first one stand, walks out to the woman's nest. She moves the nest slightly for each man so that he will not come into contact with any sexual secretions left on the grass from the earlier trysts. (Crocker and Crocker 1994:147)

With a shaped piece of wood, this woman manipulates the lips of the vagina of each girl, pulling at them, stretching them, and lightly puncturing the vaginal tissues in several places. This she does eight or nine times for each of her charges during the first year of instruction, and during the next year the girls do this for each other. . . . For two years at the very least this is continued, and in addition there is the outer massaging of these "lips" to cause thickening and muscular development, for "thin-lipped" women are considered lacking in comeliness. (Herskovits 1938:282, [cited in Murray and Roscoe 1998:264–66])

What is normal sex? The ethnographic record contains quite a wide variation in sexual behavior and customs, but are they all normal? The first passage above comes from the Sambia of New Guinea and is part of the initiation of young boys into adulthood; the second passage is about ritual sex among the Canela of the Amazon, and the third is from Dahomey (West Coast of Africa) and describes a process by which girls age 9 to 11 roughed their vaginas and lips to enhance sexual pleasure. This information alone does not tell us anything about the circumstances and motivations behind these practices. If we take them out of context, we will find it difficult to understand what cultural values and understandings drive them. To try to judge them in isolation of their surroundings puts us on unsettled ground.

Human sexuality is both embodied and *embedded*. By embedded we mean that sexual behavior is an integral part of a culture. Embodiment is a specific way of being embedded. Circumcision and blood magic are examples of both. While chapter 3 dealt with embodiment, in this chapter we deal with embedded sexuality. The idea of an embedded sexuality is intended to encourage us to see specific sexual acts and customs as related to each other and to a larger cultural and institutional organization. The chapter begins, however, by addressing the issue of sexual normality and describing some of the varieties of sexual behaviors observed cross-culturally. Because the range of potential sexual behaviors is always wider than any one culture permits, it selects some as normal and rejects others. The accepted practices become a part of organized sexuality. The resulting pattern of sexuality should not be considered static but subject to change and conflict. Change and conflict are well illustrated later in the chapter with discussions of sex and conquest, sex and slavery, and further elaborated in the concluding section on global sex.

WHAT IS NORMAL SEX?

Can there be a universally applicable measure of sexual normality that is not culture bound? An Indian sexologist and commentator on the Kama Sutra once claimed that there are 529 positions for sexual intercourse (genital to genital), but most of them are in fact simply slight postural variations on the basic ways (Gregersen 1996:62). The Perfumed Garden listed 25 Indian and 11 Arabic positions for intercourse, and Gulio Romano pictured 16 positions in his notorious etchings. Yet, for most of its history, the West considered the man on top to be the only normal position. An unknown number of Europeans no doubt found it difficult to conform to such a narrowly defined manner of activity and engaged in abnormal sex at least occasionally. In some Melanesian cultures, boys fellate men, and in the Amazon Basin, Canela women have sequential sex with a number of men. In Nepal, brothers marry one woman and sexually service her in turn. Given the wide latitude of permitted sexual behavior around the world, what can we say is normal sex? Is it whatever a culture states it to be, in which case they are all normal?

All cultures, explicitly or implicitly, define normal sexual behavior. To what extent the members of a culture actually behave according to the norm is another, related question. Statements and behavior together define norms. *Normative statements* are what people say are norms; actual behavior can be stated as a *statistical norm* for a group of people. Normative statements often, but not necessarily, have religious or moral overtones to them. Theoretically, then, each culture could make a different normative statement about sexual behavior, but in reality this is not the case. Similar cultures with a common historical background might share similar values and norms, such as Christian Europe or Islamic portions of Africa. A statistical norm results from a frequency count of actual behavior. The Kinsey reports described statistical norms for the sexual activity of men and women in the United States. These reports contributed in fact to a reconsideration of publicly stated sexual norms in the post–World War II period, because the researchers were able to document changes in actual sexual behavior that varied from the stated ideal. To develop a more complete picture of sexuality, both of these norms should be fully considered, although sexual behavior is not easily observed and must usually depend on confidential statements by individuals of their actual behavior.

What is defined as normal sex is usually also considered natural sex. The historical Christian idea of normal sex was that it should be limited to genital to genital contact for the purpose of reproduction. Pleasure was a side product not to be sought for itself. This prescribed behavior was thus defined as normal, natural, and sanctioned by the church. But a definition of normality immediately sets up opposite categories of the abnormal and unnatural for every form of sexual contact outside it. Many states in the United States have laws that define oral or anal sex as unnatural acts punishable by fines and imprisonment. Humans are capable of a wide variety of sexual behaviors unrelated to reproduction. This capacity for sexual variety is characteristic of our species and is in this sense natural.

Although humans are capable of a great variety of sexual behaviors, few of us would want to accept all of them as normal. The incest taboo is a universal rule, but it is frequently broken. The fact that we have the potential to break the rule certainly does not make it acceptable. Each society does, in fact, curb some types of sexual behavior. Unfortunately, native peoples who are sexually permissive are often stereotyped as promiscuous without limits. But they do in fact restrict some sexual activities and relationships. The *myth of primitive sexuality* is based on the false assumptions that (1) there is such a thing as primitive culture, and (2) "primitives" are closer to nature and thus give free rein to their baser animal desires in continuous and unlimited sexuality. These beliefs persist today although Malinowski showed them not to be the case with the sex-positive Trobrianders in 1929.

Sexual Positions

Coitus among humans is accomplished in a limited variety of positions (Gregersen 1996:68–70).

1. *Missionary position.* Both partners lie, face to face, with the woman below and the man on top. This position is perhaps most common cross-culturally. Western conservative religious groups often consider this the "natural" and moral position.

2. *Ur position.* The man is supine with the woman squatting on top. Traditional Western views sometimes consider this position a reflection of female dominance and male submissiveness. It is not preferred in very many cultures, but more common as a secondary position.

3. *African position.* Partners are side by side, face to face. This is said to be the preferred position in a number of African societies, and a second position in other African groups. This position can be used among older men and women, and during pregnancy. Penetration is sometimes difficult for men.

4. *Rear entry.* Man enters vagina from the rear of the woman while standing or sitting. There is a question about the reliability of reports on this position, but it does occur. Good during pregnancy. Carries with it a hint of bestiality.

5. *Oceanic position.* The man kneels between a woman's legs while she is supine, and pulls her toward him. Common in the pacific and described by Malinowski for the Trobrianders. It facilitates sex with a partner who is considered less attractive in age or beauty because little body contact is required, although easily accomplished if desired.

6. *Man sitting, women squatting, face to face.* This position is not commonly reported.

7. *Standing.* This position is mostly associated with quick, elicit affairs.

Reliable data on these practices is understandably difficult for a researcher to gain, because observation is not usually possible. Generally these findings probably are accurate at the level of normative statement in the ethnographic present. Naming sexual positions after geographical-cultural areas risks stereotyping sexuality for these regions. They are included here because they have gained some currency in discussions of cross-cultural sexuality among Western scholars.

Masturbation is common in many cultures among both sexes. In general, childhood masturbation is not considered a problem even when it is not encouraged. Historically, in Western society, it is a practice that has been condemned on religious, moral, and medical grounds. The religious and moral constraints on male masturbation come from the Judeo-Christian background with strictures against spilling one's seed: in other words, not turning sexuality to the reproductive enterprise and therefore wasting seed. Tissot connected, erroneously, masturbation to insanity, and others thought that it caused other physical maladies. Dr. J. H. Kellogg (1852–1943) believed that masturbation could be controlled by diet, especially by his corn flakes breakfast cereal (Walters 1974). In the United States, almost everyone reportedly masturbates at one time or another, although men appear to do it more than women. Those men and women with a higher education masturbate more than those with less, and those men and women with no religious affiliation more than those with affiliation (Lauman et al. 1994:82). Women are much more likely to achieve orgasm through masturbation than through sexual intercourse. Masturbation is generally accompanied by fantasizing or by viewing sexually arousing images.

Same-Sex Erotic Relationships

In this section we center our discussion on five questions: (1) What is the incidence of same-sex erotic relationships across cultures and though time? (2) Are such relationships best explained by biological or cultural factors? (3) How closely do our common labels and categories match the reality of same-sex erotic relationships? (4) What cultural meanings do we assign cross-culturally to these sexual practices and relationships? (5) How do these relationships fit into local cultural contexts?

The facts of same-sex erotic interactions are that they are present in our closest living relatives, chimps, and other mammals; they are present in humans since ancient times; and they are present cross-culturally. They are present in children in early sex play and in adults in limited contexts or in lasting relationships. They are present in males and females who do not self-identify as homosexual. The range of such interactions on the other hand is not unlimited. Stephen Murray and Will Roscoe (1998:6–9) identify three common patterns of same-sex relationships: *egalitarian*, where class, age, or race is not a formal basis for the relationship; *age stratified*, based on a difference in age or gender status (sexually receptive males are often boys or adolescents and may be categorized as being other than male); and *gender based* where the "active" male is considered male, not homosexual, and the penetrated male is given a distinct identity. Age stratified relationships are found particularly in Melanesia (and in ancient Greece), gender based relationships occur especially in the Mediterranean and Latin America. These patterns of interaction do not exclude other forms of same-sex erotic behavior but identify only the most common types. Egalitarian relationships are becoming more visible in all of these regions.

The number of homosexuals estimated for the U.S. population varies according to which source is consulted but ranges from about 2 to 10 percent. The Kinsey study revealed in the 1950s that there were more male–male experiences than female–female and that there were varying frequencies of occurrence through the life cycle, although they were especially prevalent during childhood. Childhood is a time of sexual exploration not necessarily involving identity formation. Data—including cross-cultural data—for the proportion of individuals in a culture with a homosexual identity consistently turn up percentages at about 5 or less. Cross-cultural data on homosexual experience generally are slightly higher.

Discussions of same-sex desires inevitably raise questions of body versus culture, that is, whether a biological determinist or cultural constructionist view best explains the presence of such desires. The former position suggests an inherited *essential*, or core, sexual identity, and the latter posits that sexuality has more to do with cultural meanings and personal experiences. In their introduction to *Female Desires*, Evelyn Blackwood and Saskia Wieringa (1999:16) note that while they themselves do not agree on how much weight to give each side, they do agree that there is "no sexual desire outside of a cultural ontology that mediates between bodies and culture, and there is no culture that is disembodied." Consistent with the view of this text, they reject such an either/or mode of thinking about same-sex desire. Neither body nor culture should be ignored but seen as interactive. "Deviant desires" are embedded in social relationships and cultural meanings, whatever their origin.

Upon the broad spectrum of observed sexual relationships we impose labels by which we attempt to identify and categorize the participants. Labels and categories themselves change cross-culturally and historically. The use of the term *homosexual* and its designation as an abnormal desire emerged in the West in the 1800s from the writings of the medical and psychiatric professions in Europe, which also constructed meanings of the female body and its functions (Foucault 1978; Martin 1987). Through the many decades since then the label has become its own reality. It has entered the realm of "received knowledge," unexamined knowledge that we assume accurately reflects reality. This is true as well for labels such as *gay* and *lesbian*. In their examination of "lesbian," Blackwood and Wieringa find that it does not fit well with reality. Indeed what women do together sexually may not even qualify as sex in some cultures. For example, the Lesotho (Africa) have a saying, "no penis, no sex" (Kendall 1999:228–29). Lesotho women have erotic relationships with each other, but these women are not identified as homosexuals. In the United States, in the 1800s, many women had "romantic friendships" that were generally considered to be devoid of sex, and they were not identified as homosexuals (D'Emilio and Freedman 1997:121).

Western categories of homosexuality and heterosexuality do not match the complex reality of behaviors, desires, and identities that we observe in a variety of cultural contexts. Our terminology is too rigid and dichotomous. We are, in Serena Nanda's (2000:1) terms, thinking in "binary opposites" when we try to hammer the variety of experiences into one set of opposing terms, homosexual or heterosexual. While the male/female distinction is a basic human idea, sex and gender do not cleave so cleanly in various cultures. Nanda (2000:1) tries to capture the variety of labels that exist in the term gender diversity. Other cultures do not, in contrast to the West, make sexual orientation the essence of individual identity. Consequently, a person involved in same-sex erotic relationships might escape receiving a distinctive label because sex is not an important criterion for social classification. We find, however, that there is much more to labeling and defining than just mislabeling reality. The ability to name and categorize implies the power to impose this "reality" on others. Ignorance can certainly figure in mislabeling, but knowledge can be ignored if other motives trump it.

Europeans early in the colonization of Africa created the myth that homosexuality does not exist there (Roscoe and Murray 1998). They considered Africans to be among the most primitive people, closest to nature and therefore because of their "natural" state they had to be heterosexual. If anything, Africa was popularly pictured as a continent of lusty men and hot women who needed to be saved from themselves by civilized Christians. Various writers on the African scene, including anthropologists, therefore ignored homosexual practices throughout most of the twentieth century.

Alfred Kinsey (1953:488) tried to avoid binary thinking by constructing a continuum of sexuality that represents degrees of heterosexual and homosexual experience among the U.S. public sampled by him and his colleagues. Few people in U.S. surveys identify themselves as bisexual (1 percent), but more (4 percent) say that they have been sexually attracted to both sexes. It has been suggested that some homosexuals are hiding behind the bisexual label, and others have suggested that bisexuality just reflects sexual experimentation rather than an identity. Nor do women in non-Western cultures, who are interested in same-sex relationships, necessarily conform to a Western model of "butch" and "femme," that is, a homosexual pair must be comprised of a male woman and a female woman (this binary formulation doesn't necessarily work in the United States either). At the same time, there is much evidence that Western terminologies are beginning to influence categories and identities in other cultures (see "Global Sex," later in this chapter).

Same-sex erotic relationships are categorized and labeled differently in different cultures, and they also carry different meanings. Meaning refers to how they are valued, identified, and understood. *Woman–woman marriages* occur in more than 30 African groups (Carrier and Murray 1998:255), and are usually related closely to status, property, and inheritance (see chapter 5) and not sexuality. Meanings might vary within a culture. Azande (Central Africa) princes had sexual relations with boys, or pages, because they liked them, or because women were taboo at times (Murray and Roscoe 1998:26–28). Azande warriors formed relations with *boy-wives* (an age-stratified pattern), even if they had female wives, and would take the boys with them during wars. They reportedly satisfied themselves sexually between the boys' thighs. Boy-wives grew up to do the same. Both of these practices disappeared when wars ceased and the social structure changed.

Nanda writes that not only do her case studies demonstrate linguistically *marked* (reflected in language use) sex/gender variations, but they also show that the variations are an *integral, institutionalized* part of the culture. An important part of the meaning of same-sex relationships lies in how they are integrated into society. Nanda's work with the Hijra of India, for example, indicates them to be located in a religious, hierarchal, and patriarchal context. They nevertheless occupy an ambiguous identity and people are ambivalent about them. "Individuals who do not fit into society's major sex/gender categories may be stigmatized but may find, within Hinduism, meaningful and valued gender identifications" (p. 28). In the United States, a number of Native American cultures had people known as *berdache*. Nanda notes that this is a pejorative word that comes from the Arabic and was used by Europeans to label men who dressed and acted like women and had sex with men (2000:11). These individuals actually occupied different roles in different cultures. Because the label covers a wide variety of behaviors and beliefs, it is inadequate as well as biased (Roscoe 1998). The term *two-spirit* has gained some currency lately as a satisfactory, if not perfect, replacement. Richard Trexler (1995) explores the varying roles of the *berdache* throughout the Americas and exposes the ethnocentrism and the associations that the European conquerors constructed between gendered violence and conquest.

Melanesian cultures offer an interesting case study of homosexual behavior that blurs the distinction between homosexuality and heterosexuality and exemplifies the age-stratified pattern. Homosexual experience is integrated into these cultures as both normal and necessary. The Sambia are but one of the societies in which ritual homosexuality occurs as an integral part of becoming a man. In these Pacific island groups, a careful, even antagonistic, distance is maintained between males and females; men must maintain their individual and collective strength in order to defend against the enemy. Some of these cultures feature *phallic cults*, where boys and young men are ritually inseminated by older men in the belief that to do so makes the young ones strong with male essence. Gilbert Herdt (1981:8) estimates that 10 to 20 percent of the groups in the Melanesian area historically practiced this form of initiation and sexual development. Most no longer do because of culture change. Herdt (1981, 1987) believes that, for the Sambia at least, this is a demonstration of masculinity that reflects some of their own fears, one being that women are really the more powerful sex.

The Sambia demonstrate why it is important to separate from each other *erotic desire, practice*, and *identity*. The Sambia do not identify themselves as homosexuals, although they pass through a period of homosexual practice. Indeed, they use the phallic cult as a way to make men of boys whom they fear are too influenced by women in the boys' early years. This practice has to be to some degree homoerotic for the men because erection is achieved. However, some boys must be forced to fellate against their desire. Occasionally there are a few (less than 5 percent) who wish to continue homosexual practices once they reach the heterosexual stage. The meaning of homosexual experience in this case clearly differs from its meaning in Western culture.

PATTERNS OF SEXUALITY

In his discussion of adult sexuality, Malinowski ([1929]1987) notes that there are various seasons and festivities that stimulate eroticism. The festivities include picnics, games, bathing parties, and certain ceremonial occasions. The appearance of the full moon and associated activities, games, and festivals, stimulate erotic interest. Trobriand games are not sexual games, but they contain a sexual element. For example, body contact in the context of rhythmic music and an attitude of frivolity where ribald rhymes are shouted between the two sexes can lead later to sexual activity. Hide-and-seek offers opportunities for individuals to be alone with each other as a preliminary sexual foray leading to love-making. Married women are not allowed to play this game. Hide-and-seek is played when the cooling trade winds blow, making it too uncomfortable for the bathing parties that are popular in warmer times.

The harvest festivals are conducive to erotic connections because people are in a joyous mood, and the young have much freedom as they travel on social walks to other villages carrying gifts of food. Men and women adorn themselves in the most attractive fashion. Women are sometimes aggressive in sexual matters. They arrange their own amorous expeditions to other villages if they think that the males in their own village are too occupied with other matters such as fishing and long-distance trading. If the women accept gifts from young men in the village, they are also accepting them as lovers that night, usually to the chagrin of the local women. These trysts are conducted privately with decorum and are not in anyway orgiastic.

The Trobianders do not kiss, although in foreplay the mouth is used extensively: They do touch tongues and lips, and rub lips together. They bite the cheek and nose, pull each other's hair, and scratch each other to draw blood. The scratch marks are, of course, fully open to view and draw jokes from observers. Biting off eye lids was also quite common. The Trobianders do not like the "missionary position," with the man on top, as commonly practiced by Westerners. The women also complain that Western men achieve orgasm too quickly. (They had contact with Western sailors, missionaries, and other outsiders for at least fifty years before Malinowski's arrival among them.)

In these and other passages, Malinowski fully describes an accepted sexuality anchored securely in its larger cultural setting. He describes a pattern of sexuality. *A sex pattern is a normative set of sexual behaviors, values, and meanings held and practiced in a particular cultural context.* The concept requires a broad, systematic, context-sensitive description and analysis of sexuality embedded in time and place. Thus, Malinowski constructed out of his observations and interviews a sex pattern, a descriptive model, of Trobriand sexuality. A descriptive model or sex pattern does not assume that everyone fits comfortably into the established pattern. It is only a beginning, a baseline picture of sexuality, that does not preclude eventual expansion into a more complex pattern of alternative sexualities. Nor does a descriptive model assume an unchanging and unchallenged pattern frozen in time. Remember that Trobriand females had already had sex with outsiders before Malinowski arrived. In addition to describing sex values and practices, a descriptive model must trace their relationship to other aspects of culture, for example, gender, marriage, and morality.

The Canela, in the Brazilian Amazon of South America, exhibit another pattern of sexuality. As one element of their pattern, they specify a time at which they engage in sequential sex. It is a feature that lends itself easily to sexual stereotyping by outsiders as typical of a "primitive" culture. After boys have gained some sexual experience, they must have sequential sex with women at the Wild Boar ceremonies. However, there is only one man with a woman at any one time, and the event does not last long. Attendance at this ceremony is compulsory for boys, and although the girls are expected to participate, and most do, they are not required to do so. Once the boys mature a bit, their participation is no longer required. Both boys and girls are socialized for this experience by the sexual joking and general atmosphere underscoring the fun of sex. They learn not to be stingy with their partners. Moreover, they are having sequential sex with others whom they know and with whom they have joked all of their lives. Women will have sex with their classificatory husbands (men who are considered husbands in addition to the "real" husband) for the rest of their lives. Jealousy does occur occasionally but is counteracted by group pressure. A man who is stingy with his wife will be taught a lesson when he is away and his wife is taken for sequential sex and returned without the customary gifts that accompany the act. He is thereby reminded of the values by which the Canela live. Canela sexuality is controlled, however, by certain defined occasions, by the relationships among the participants, and by other restrictions such as blood taboos.

Sequential sex, as well as extramarital sex, among the Canela is within certain limitations accepted, valued, and prepared for in child rearing, and therefore is institutionalized. In their treatment of the human problems that accompany sexual access to more than one person—jealousy, potential violence, and disruption of important social relations—the Canela have minimized, but not eliminated, sources of conflict. Indeed they use sex as a "mending way." Sexual activity is an important form of communication among social entities such as opposite age classes and classificatory husbands. It fosters solidarity rather than driving apart these social groups. Because younger women have sex with older men, it fosters intergenerational ties.

We study sexuality in small-scale societies represented by the Canela and the Trobrianders because they provide us with focused examples of a relatively uniform sex pattern that guides individual sexuality. Ultimately, these case studies yield an unrealistic and static image of sexuality. In fact, such a model no longer accurately reflects the situation that the Canela and Trobrianders find themselves in today, and it certainly is inadequate for understanding sexuality in the modern world. Nor is a static model adequate to cope with a large and complex society like the United States. In the remainder of this chapter, we further develop our understanding of sexuality in cultural context by examining the topics of sex and conquest, sexual revolution in the United States, and global sex. The case studies presented in the next section underscore two elements that are critical to developing a more sophisticated model of sexuality—*change* and *conflict*.

SEX AND CONQUEST

Interracial Sexual Contact in Early America

The North American colonies did not share a common sex pattern. The Pilgrims arrived in New England determined to carve out a new life in the wilderness by hard work and pious living. They are usually depicted as being puritanical about sex, but they accepted the role of sexual intercourse in solidifying the family and producing children as long as it was practiced in moderation. Because of the high infant mortality rate, women were often pregnant, which assumes a certain frequency of intercourse. As long as the intent was to produce children, sex was acceptable. The Pilgrims strictly forbid extramarital sex, although it happened occasionally. Although premarital sex was also forbidden, it was not unusual and nothing was said as long as the couple married before a child was born, an idea they brought with them from England (D'Emilio and Freedman 1997:8). Although they valued the role of the individual in religious and practical matters, they were extremely vigilant against sexual transgressors who threatened the unity of the group.

The settlers of Southern colonies of the Chesapeake region shared with those Northern colonies most of the same values about sex, but they experienced a different way of life. Their sex patterns were therefore different. Whereas New England life was town-centered and cohesive, Southern life was based on scattered farms and a more unstable family life. Men outnumbered women by four to one (D'Emilio and Freedman 1997:10), and there were some interracial marriages before prohibitions were enacted against them in the late 1600s. Adultery may have been more prevalent because women were in such demand that they could always find another husband. Community surveillance of sexual contact was less strict because farms were widely dispersed. While the settlers in New England were a homogeneous group seeking religious freedom, those in the South came from more widely disparate backgrounds and had a more pragmatic economic purpose (p. 11).

These two patterns of sexuality were not the only ones present on the frontier. Both regions also had to contend with the presence of Native Americans whom both groups perceived to practice a sexuality quite different from theirs and, in fact, to constitute a threat to the colonial agenda. The colonials made sex and marriage, with religion, the key practices that separated civilized people from "savages."

Mary White Rowlandson was taken captive by the Narrangasetts in 1676 during King Philip's War in Massachusetts. She was ransomed from captivity three months later. In 1682, she published a narrative of her experience, the first prose written by an American woman (although she referred to herself as English) (Faery 1999:24). Her story served as a template for the numerous stories about captive white women that followed. It is that template that captures our interest here.

Pocahontas (Powhatan tribe) was detained in Jamestown for three years from 1613 to 1616. She was perhaps fifteen years old when she was "captured" and was already married to another Powhatan, named Kocoum. Although legend has it that she instantly fell in love with John Smith and saved him from certain death at the hands of the Narrangasetts, the evidence is sketchy. What is clear is that she married John Rolfe, and that they traveled to England where she died in 1617, leaving one child from her union with Rolfe.

Rebecca Faery argues that Rowlandson and Pocahontas are inextricably part of a narrative about sex, Christianity and conquest; they represent two sides of the same coin.

> Those endless circulating tales of captivity, however, not only helped to construct Indians as a distinct racial group, with the bodies and sexuality of white women captives as the contested zone, they also served a larger purpose: the narratives contained epic elements in that the captive's story became the story of the colonial, and later national, culture itself. (1999:40)

In the early history of the New England borderlands, the bodies of Pocahontas and Mary Rowlandson became contested symbols of cultural and racial difference. The colonial authorities, religious and civil, needed to make use of these bodies. Pocahontas had to be an exceptional rather than typical, virginal (although already married), Indian woman who had to be "dislodged" from her culture to accept English culture (Faery 1999:103). Mary Rowlandson, on the other hand, was a mature, married woman with children when captured. The lingering question upon her return from captivity, and one that had to be preempted, was whether she had been raped. She did not explicitly answer that question in her book (or elsewhere apparently), but instead a male writer of the preface emphasized her gentleness and piety to forestall embarrassing questions. Rowlandson's story had to be framed as a threat to colonization and as a parable about the Puritan's struggle against the devil (Faery 1999:41). White female purity had to be saved.

The colonists did not see interracial sexual contact as a mere byproduct of frontier interactions, but as a threat to the colonial enterprise—one that needed to be commented on, and one that needed powerful symbols to mediate what they considered to be profound differences. They saw Indian women as promiscuous and dangerously attractive and Indian men as potential rapists. God-fearing, civilized white people should persevere in the face of the Indian challenge to their way of life. Pocahontas was made into a good Indian by becoming Christian and civilized.

Other colonies in North America shared the same concerns about the progress of colonization that the New Englanders did. In the Carolinas in the 1700s, those who regularly traveled on the margins of civilization often had contact with the Indians, some of it sexual. "As travelers, traders, soldiers, and diplomats dealt with Native Americans on what one historian has called the middle ground, their interaction, accommodations, cultural misunderstandings were as much sexual as they were economic, diplomatic, and military" (Godbeer 1999:92). Traders were often on the trails for long periods of time and would arrange for sexual and domestic services from Indian women (p. 91). As in New England, Carolinian authorities saw such arrangements as potential threats to the progress of colonization. They wrongly assumed that all Indian cultures approved of sexual experimentation, which was not the case. They also misinterpreted gift exchange as prostitution rather than an integral part of Indian life.

French Louisiana, in the early 1700s, suffered from a problem common in frontier areas: a scarce supply of women. The men would leave the French community to visit the Indian women in their villages, and the colonial administrators feared the French men would not return from the villages to carry on their work. The colonial administrators saw sexual interaction between French men and Indian women as a threat to colony building (Spear 1999). The administration constructed Indian sexuality as being promiscuous. Even divorce was accomplished too easily. Administrators therefore mounted a campaign to import more women from France to keep the men away from the Indian women. Missionaries, in contrast to colonial administrators, saw interracial marriages as a way to convert Indians to Christianity.

Interracial sex and marriage in the colonies was not just about whites and Indians, or whites and blacks. Runaway slaves frequently found refuge, sexual outlet, and marriage in Indian communities. Black men had something more to gain by marrying Indian women. First, Indian women could sometimes purchase their husband's freedom, and their children would be free whether or not the men were free. Second, the men could gain access to land and to a community that they could not have done otherwise (Mandell 1999:79). The case of Sara Muckamugg brings us back to interracial marriage in New England. Sara was a Nipmuc Indian who lived in Massachusetts. In 1728, she married a black slave named Aaron, but was divorced twelve years later. She then married another black slave, Fortune Burnee (Mandell 1999).

At this time, New England seaports were prospering and drawing workers from rural precincts. As a result, blacks and Indians often found themselves working together. Indians worked at unskilled jobs, while blacks worked as laborers, carpenters, seamen, and house servants (Mandell 1999:73). Both groups were considered to be at the bottom of the social ladder. In addition, the demographic profile of the two populations created a "complementary imbalance." The Indian population had too many women, and the black population had too many men. Given this imbalance, and an opportunity for social equals to meet, the presence of interracial marriage is not a surprising result.

Religious beliefs of the colonists were often undermined by an unbalanced sex ratio and the conditions under which local populations worked. Social standing influenced sexual and marital decision making and the degree to which sexual variations were monitored or punished.

Sex and Slavery

The sexual and family life of slaves was severely controlled by white plantation owners before the Civil War and by other measures after the war. The Southern colonies raised racial barriers to interracial sex and marriage, *miscegenation*, by the end of the 1600s. White planters were generally not constrained by these sexual prohibitions and often formed sexual unions with black slave women regardless of whether or not the women desired it. Black women often resisted white owners and tried various evasive maneuvers, which were at least partly successful sometimes (Block 1999). Although rare, white women did sometimes have sex with black men, but in doing so risked extreme ostracism if they had any status, even if they escaped legal consequences; the black men risked severe punishment, even death.

Slavery exerted extreme pressure on the ability of slaves to maintain stable families; it was in fact illegal for them to marry. Families could be broken up by selling individual members to other plantations because bodies were owned by the planters to do with as they saw fit. Restrictions were sometimes imposed on common residence. Yet slaves often achieved stable and enduring unions. Even when separated, couples tried to remain in contact with each other. Sexual pleasures were linked to reproduction. Premarital sex, which is a meaningless concept when marriage is illegal, was permitted.

At issue in miscegenation was the institution of slavery and racial order. Interracial marriage could undermine the established social order and therefore was prohibited. Children of mixed ancestry "blurred the sharply demarcated boundaries" (Bardaglio 1999:113) between the "races." The laws were enacted to keep blacks in their place and to protect the purity of white women. These goals "reflected the degree to which the structure of power in the South rested on both gender and racial classification" (p. 113). Such rigid regimes of control produced negative effects in both populations. "The sexual exploitation of slaves disrupted the family life of both races, giving all women reason to condemn the practice" (p. 116). Black men on their part were powerless to protect their women and felt diminished because of it.

During Reconstruction, after the Civil War, the Southern states moved swiftly to restore racial order by passing new laws, many of which still prohibited miscegenation. Weapons of terror, principally rape and lynching, supported Jim Crow (laws of segregation) in an effort to keep African Americans in their place. Between 1889 and 1940, over 3,800 African Americans were lynched in the South and border states. In addition, the segregationists pushed the myth of the loose and lustful black woman and the crazed black man who craved white women. Black men in fact rarely raped white women (D'Emilio and Freedman 1997:37), and most of the lynchings were carried out in retaliation against black men who had attempted to protect their families from white rapists or against blacks who were becoming too successful. These tactics were designed to keep former slaves in their place and lasted well into the twentieth century.

White men raped black women as another act of terrorism. The violence directed against black women was an important impetus for the creation of the National Association for the Advancement of Colored People (NAACP) in 1910 (D'Emilio and Freedman 1997:219). Many black women soon joined together for mutual protection and political action. The myth of the lustful black woman and the sexually aggressive black man did not die a quick death. The image of a black, lustful savage assaulting a civilized, innocent white woman was purveyed to a wide audience in D. W. Griffith's silent film classic, *The Birth of a Nation*.

THE SEXUAL REVOLUTION

The nineteenth century witnessed fundamental changes in North American lifestyles and sexuality. Economic, social, and political forces played instrumental roles in shaping the direction of change, but as always in cases of change, more conservative groups resisted some of the new developments, especially with respect to sexual practices. During this century, the size of the family shrank, the roles of men and women changed, sex education gained a foothold, and improved contraception became more widely available. Slavery was abolished, but after the Civil War white authorities enacted segregation laws and revitalized old sexual myths in order to control African Americans. The sexual revolution refers usually to the 1960s and '70s, but it is important to understand some of the key changes that took place earlier, and, in fact, set the stage for the revolution.

Young men in the rural areas in the 1800s increasingly saw their future in the burgeoning cities and developing industries of North America. They took jobs that paid them wages but also removed them from their homes for much of the day. Women remained at home to do household chores and tend children. Men began to see new economic opportunities in the business and industrial expansion, as well as a way to join the middle class. Men were told that to be successful in the new competitive environment they must control their nature. They were told to conserve their precious, competitive energy by abstaining from masturbation. A man in control of himself was in control of his future.

Women were told that they were to be sexually pure—they were not really interested in sex by nature—and spiritual. They were sent this message by way of male "authorities" on women and marriage in the form of sermons and early marriage manuals. Yet, men and women were also becoming more explicitly romantic and less pragmatic about such matters as economic support and property. Their letters and diaries revealed more romantic passion and sexual experience (not necessarily coitus) (D'Emilio and Freedman 1997:76).

In the beginning of the nineteenth century, families tended to be large in order to have a sufficiently large number of workers to make farms a success. The white reproduction rate was over seven children per family at the beginning of the 1800s but fell to four by 1880 (D'Emilio and Freedman 1997:58). As labor-saving machinery was developed for farm use, displaced sons of farmers headed for the city. Those working in cities for wage labor produced smaller families. Economic pressures in the direction of smaller families were joined by better sex education and improved contraceptive techniques, although both were available more to middle-class families than to those in the lower class. The Philadelphia Exposition introduced condoms in 1878, followed soon by the diaphragm.

Contraceptive devices were eagerly sought and widely distributed through the U.S. mail system, along with literature about sex. Sexual literature provided more than practical advice on sexual matters; it also advanced the idea that sexual satisfaction is important to the quality of personal life, and it recognized women as sexual beings. Margaret Sanger's crusade in the early 1900s on the behalf of birth control further boosted implicitly the fact of female sexual desire. Birth control gave women some control over their bodies and some relief from the undesired results of male sexual pressures. Sanger, in fact, became a crusader partly to give women control over their bodies but also because she was appalled by the horrors of back-alley abortions and unwanted children among lower-class families. The emerging popularity of contraception alarmed Congress as it feared that such devices would encourage sexual adventure beyond the family and that sexual matters would begin to spin out of public control. They envisioned rampant sexuality undermining the effectiveness of practical work. Subsequently, Congress passed the Comstock law (1873) that prohibited the use of the postal system to distribute contraceptive devices and information.

The sexual mores of the twentieth century little resembled those of the Pilgrims. Bridging them are the transitional changes of the 1800s, which formed the platform from which sprang further and more radical changes in the 1960s and '70s. John Heidenry (1997:20) considers the sexual revolution to be part of a "permanent continuum of revolutionary events" and that it is really just beginning. For Heidenry, the sexual revolution began with the birth of sexology in Austria and Germany in the late 1800s, gained momentum during the 1920s, and exploded in the 1960s (p. 12). Although he focuses on the

1960s and '70s, he believes that the fourth stage will be driven by modern technology and engulf the world. He traces four "narrative strands" of development: sex research, pornography, sexual minorities, and sexual culture (meanings, values, and beliefs). The following narrative also includes those strands (although sexology was covered in the first chapter), but they are interwoven with other strands and covered also in other chapters of this text.

Celia Mosher and Katherine B. Davis are two important sex researchers not mentioned in the opening chapter. Near the end of the 1800s, Mosher (1980)[1] surveyed 45 Victorian women born between 1850 and 1880 and found that sexual experience in marriage was best for women when a "spirit of mutuality" prevailed (D'Emilio and Freedman 1997:80). Many of them still felt that reproduction is the main purpose of sex, and some professed not to be particularly interested in it as source of satisfaction. Davis (1929) surveyed 1,000 women who were old enough to marry prior to World War I. Most of them, in fact, were born before 1890. Seventy percent of the women in the Davis study practiced some form of contraception, while a larger proportion believed that its use was morally right and that other reasons than procreation justified sexual expression (p. 75). The studies yielded results that were consistent with each other in many ways. They both revealed that, by and large, women believed that sex was agreeable but were sometimes conflicted between old and new ways. Most of them had received little or no sex education.

Because of increasing worry over a spurt in the incidence of venereal disease, various social hygiene movements sprung up. The National Education Association endorsed sex education as early as 1912, but actually launched programs much later. States began to require blood tests before issuing a marriage license in an effort to control sexually transmitted diseases. Sanger's birth control movement was under way by then as well. One of the results of this convergence of interests was to drive deeper the wedge between sex for pleasure and sex for reproduction.

The "roaring twenties" continued the trend toward a loosening of sexual behavior. The looser lifestyle included women wearing form-fitting clothing, smoking cigarettes, and having dates. With the coming of the thirties came the speak-easy and further efforts by parents to use birth control measures to keep families small. World War II preoccupied the nation until 1945, after which came both a population boom and changing economic circumstances, events that did not necessarily benefit all segments of the population. The repressive and placid fifties idolized the "traditional" family with the wife as "homemaker" as symbolized in the television show, *Leave It to Beaver.*

The sexual revolution did not burst on the United States in a vacuum. Dramatic challenges to mainstream sexuality mirrored other assaults on the values and institutional structure of society. Sexual tumult coexisted with student protests, political assassinations, and general public turmoil. Discontent and activism erupted in many areas of life, leaving a confused and resistant public. One of the first shots of the revolution was fired by Hugh Heffner who published his first issue of *Playboy* magazine in late 1953, in the decade of relative calm. The first edition featured the nude calendar photos of Marilyn Monroe. The magazine proved to be so successful that Heffner appeared on the cover of *Time* magazine. He bought a 100-room mansion in Chicago and hosted nightly parties that usually ended in sex orgies (Heidenry 1997:61). Although much of the appeal of the magazine lay in its nude photos of women, it also featured essays, literature, and criticism. Perhaps most important it served as a vehicle to spread sexual freedom. *Playboy* eventually reached a peak circulation of about six million. It was followed in the 1960s by *Penthouse*, created by Bob Guccione, who thought Heffner to be too conservative and became his arch rival, and *Hustler*, published by Larry Flynt, who thought that both *Playboy* and *Penthouse* were too conservative. The plays, *Hair* and *Oh Calcutta* introduced to the stage nudity and sexually explicit language. By the 1970s, pornographic movies, such as *Deep Throat*, were playing in Main Street theaters across the nation.

The new sexual freedom was joined by new knowledge of sexual function that was to have a divisive impact for a while on the second wave of feminism (the first wave occurred in the beginning of the century). Helen Gurley Brown's *Sex and the Single Girl* (1962) encouraged women to remain single and to use men for sexual pleasure. The women's movement sought to convince women to take control of their bodies and their sexuality, a mindset that contrasted with those implied by images of women featured in male-oriented magazines. Added to the mix was pornography, which often contained scenes where women were not in control of their bodies, but were being sexually used, sometimes violently. Some feminists argued for censorship, while others argued that though they found such scenes degrading they could not accept censorship of them because of their belief in the First Amendment. In addition, they wanted to be careful not to give up the hard-won fact that women have sexual desire (see chapter 6 for more on this controversy).

In 1966, William Masters and Virginia Johnson proved that female orgasm is triggered by the clitoris, not the vagina. Many feminists had long argued that vaginal orgasm is a male myth because it required a penis to give satisfaction to a woman. Most women knew very well that orgasm is based on the clitoris and requires no penetration. The male, in fact, is not needed at all for orgasm. The Hite Report (1976) on female sexuality provided further anecdotal evidence for the clitoral orgasm and indicated further that masturbation usually produced the strongest orgasm.

By the 1980s, sex had lost much of its moral underpinning. More couples cohabited without censure, and more adolescents were having sex. More couples performed fellatio and cunnilingus. Nevertheless, a conservative backlash was building as Ronald Reagan became president with the blessings of the "moral majority." Today, in spite of the fact that American culture is sexually saturated, we appear still to be uneasy about our private and public sexuality. John Heidenry (1997:413–14) considers the sexual revolution to be a failure because it did not relieve us of our guilt and anxiety over sexual pleasure, and because the West remains polarized on the issue of sexuality.

GLOBAL SEX

The phrase, "global village," has now gained common currency throughout the world. It refers to the interlacing international ties that actually began thousands of years ago in ancient trade routes and empire building and reached a new level of international interdependency in recent decades. The ease of air travel, a proliferation of international corporations, and the explosion in mass communication have combined to facilitate the growth of today's densely webbed ties. International dialogue concerning the opportunities and the problems that the global village presents focuses mostly on the political, economic, and cultural dimensions, and less on the sexual dimension that ultimately also has political, economic, and cultural relevance. Sex, Dennis Altman (2001) argues, ought to be treated like a business (see Heidenry 1997 for a similar view). *Global sex* is an international business and bears international and national political ramifications. This section discusses global sex in general, while more specific issues with global dimensions are treated in succeeding chapters as appropriate.

Four areas of global sex garner much of the media discussion: sex tourism, the HIV/AIDS pandemic, the trade in children for sex, and pornography via the Internet. As Altman (2001) observes, it is easy to be morally indignant about these practices, but it is too often an "historically uninformed" reaction that fails to move from the initial moral position to a deeper understanding. In other words, these sexual issues should not be treated in isolation, but as a part of larger economic, political, and cultural forces at work.

Globalization challenges local customs and institutions, advocates scientific knowledge and business principles, and spreads Western, especially North American, culture. Although nations are not incapable of resisting the introduction of Euroamerican culture, or even disseminating their own, the demands of globalization exert enormous pressure on local populations. Changes in sexual values, behavior, and identity are evident around the world (Altman 2001:34) as a part of the changing political economy. Altman, for example, observes that "sex is a central part of large cities, especially those which are growing fast, and therefore home to many who are uprooted, transient, desperate—or newly rich in times of political or social upheaval" (p. 11). These cities also exhibit rapidly expanding commercial sex operations. Russian and Chinese cities, since the collapse of communism and the "triumph" of capitalism, are examples where the increase in commercial sex has been spawned by dramatic turns in the political economy of these nations. Perhaps a half-million women in Soviet/Eastern Europe were imported into western Europe for prostitution between 1995 and 1998.

Sex tourism is big business in Thailand and brings into the national treasury enormous sums of cash (see chapter 6). In his concluding paragraph on the Thai sex industry, Jeremy Seabrook (1996:169–170) observes:

> It is a savage irony that sex tourism should be one symptom of globalization, the "integration" of the whole world into a single economy, when both the workers in the industry and the clients from abroad are themselves the product of disintegration—of local communities, the dissolution of rootedness and belonging, the breaking of old patterns of labor and traditional livelihoods, and the psychic disintegration of so many people caught up in great epic changes, of which they have little understanding and over which they have no control.

Globalization alters local institutional structures, breaks down taboos, and engenders cultural clashes and misunderstandings. It challenges group and individual identities, and often advocates sex as the defining characteristic of a person. It spreads an international youth culture with ideas of sexual experimentation and love and threatens ideas of family and community. Women are particularly at a disadvantage because they usually are more powerless (but not helpless). HIV/AIDS prevention programs introduce new classifications of sex and disease, new vocabulary, new conceptions of the body, and new values. These may be unintended consequences of globalization, but they are nevertheless real.

SUMMARY

As intellectually and emotionally complex creatures, we naturally seek sexual experiences beyond the reproductive act. Cultures define segments of the wide range of potential sexual behavior as normal and accepted. Normative standards do not stand alone, but are intertwined with the fabric of culture. By use of the term *sex pattern* we intend to understand sexual values and norms, not as isolated features, but as fully integrated with other elements of culture. Individual sex identities and desires fit into this defined pattern with varying degrees of comfort.

Erotic same-sex relationships have been a part of the human sex potential from the beginning, but they have been treated differently in different cultures. Same-sex desires and behaviors may be accepted, rejected, tolerated or ignored in a given pattern, but in any case they challenge our common understanding of them. Our common understanding is muddled by inadequate terminology and uninformed labels, but we can remedy this condition by taking the comparative perspective. Doing so undermines the binary terms *heterosexual* and *homosexual* that are common in the West.

We use sexuality in a variety of nonsexual ways. We use it to maintain group boundaries, and as an instrument of power and authority—even a terrorist technique. Sex is also of commercial value both nationally and internationally, and plays an integral role in globalization. The globalization of sex results from, and contributes to, the breakdown in traditional institutions and values.

CRITICAL INQUIRY

---

1. Try to describe a sex pattern for the United States. Is it possible to have more than one sex pattern in a culture? Into what kind of pattern do you think you best fit?

2. In what ways do you think the sexual revolution in the United States influenced you and your family? Is the sexual revolution over? Explain your answer.

3. Have you ever employed sexual stereotypes in an effort to maintain group boundaries? Can you identify any such tactics reported on by the news media?

NOTE

---

[1] Mosher's findings were not published until recently.

Chapter Five

Regulating Sex
Incest Taboos, Marriage, and Descent

Having complete freedom to scratch the sexual itch whenever desired may well be a universal fantasy, but it remains an unsatisfied one in reality. The unregulated pursuit of sexual pleasure is in fact characteristic of no culture known to us. If a state of sexual freedom did prevail at some time in our distant past, we must have discovered very early two truths: (1) free sex is not free but potentially dangerous to group life, the success of which depends on mutual cooperation; and (2) the sexual urge can be turned to collective use by attaching it to other important customs and institutions. Even the sex-positive Canelas and Trobrianders understand the limits of their sexual explorations and try to live up to community standards of sexual conduct imposed on them. As chapter 4 indicated, both groups turned sex to its collective good by enmeshing it in the web of values and institutions that form the core of their culture.

Marriage and descent are traditionally the two principal institutions cross-culturally charged with regulating sexual access. The universally expressed incest taboo that forbids sex and marriage between close relatives supports these key institutions. This chapter examines how incest, marriage, and descent organize sexuality and discusses such related topics as selecting a mate, reproduction, extramarital sex, and divorce.

COURTSHIP

Courtship preceding sexual union is characteristic of sexually re-producing species. The dancing, preening, and gift-giving courtship be-havior typically associated with nonhuman species, if successful, culmi-nates in mating behavior. Humans also conduct courtship rituals, although we might not recognize some of our behavior as such. Other species conduct their courtship and mating activities within a limited mating season, during which time males compete for a female who chooses the most fit partner from among the competitors. Humans have no defined mating season, and patterns of courtship vary consid-erably among cultures in length, kind of activity, and degree of formal-ity. Sexual interaction may be an integral part of the courtship phase or may occur at the end of it, or at the beginning of marriage. Malinowski [1929]1987:263–64) notes several direct approaches to courtship used by the Trobrianders: (1) A man and woman can speak directly to each other about their feelings. (2) They can use an intermediary if there is a great geographical distance involved; a friend of the boy in such a case speaks to the girl. (3) They may use love magic. Because the Trobrian-ders believe that all love can ultimately be attributed to magic, this in their view can be the most effective approach.

The eye play and body dance that humans engage in, hoping to create a relationship, is *flirting*. Through a series of exchanges—body language, gazes, and verbal games—potential partners try to assess the extent of their interest in each other. Flirting may or may not be a part of courtship, but certainly is common across cultures. It is this kind of behavior that some Islamic peoples try to avoid by putting women in robes and veils. Ethologists, those who observe creatures in their natural habitat, such as Eibl-Eibesfeldt (1989), have observed flirting behavior in humans cross-culturally and found similarities in flirting behavior that do not seem to be culture bound. Timothy Perper (1985), a biologist, and David Givens (1983), an anthropologist, ob-served flirting as a part of "pick-up" strategies in singles bars. Flirting can also be an expression of dominance and authority. Kevin Yelving-ton (2001) observed flirting patterns at a Trinidadian (in the Carib-bean Ocean) factory between female workers of African or East Indian descent and white supervisors. He reports that "flirting is not only an idiom for expressing one's sexuality and sexual desire, but it is also an instrument for exercising (and resisting) power along various axes" (p. 221). Flirting in this case enacts, or reproduces, the structure of power among unequal relationships.

In general, mate selection through courtship can be classified as to the degree to which it is *autonomous* or *arranged* (Pasternak, Em-

ber, and Ember 1997:151). In autonomous mate selection the princi-
pals are relatively free to choose on the basis of their romantic attachment, while arranged marriages proceed more on the basis of a family
or descent group's strategic interests. These are convenient categories
by which to organize courtship, but in reality they may merge with one
another occasionally. Mangaian men and women are not, in spite of
the permissiveness in premarital sexual adventures, free to marry just
anyone with whom they are sexually and emotionally intimate. Even
long-term romances eventually need the approval of the parents. As
the Mangaian case illustrates, courtship can begin in a self-directed
manner, but if it becomes a more stable and hence serious relationship,
parents may become increasingly involved. Group goals can supercede
romantic passion, as it has occasionally with Mangaians, causing great
individual pain and suffering—perhaps ending in suicide.

The Fulbe of North Cameroun (West Africa) see romantic passion
as a threat to social stability and believe that anyone who reveals such
a commitment in public is possessed and diseased and may even be
subjected to an exorcism.[1] Lovers desire to spend too much time
around each other and thus make themselves unavailable to others.
Because of this belief, women daily deny that they love their husbands.
The fear of public shame is a powerful deterrent to a person's display
of romantic passion. The Fulbe place a premium on social obligations.

> Availability to others, commensality, respect, deference for elders
> are expressed in Fulbe practices of eating, greeting, patterns of vis-
> iting and sitting together, and body language generally. The indi-
> vidual affirms both the egalitarian and hierarchical principles of
> the social order in his or her everyday discourse. Both of these prin-
> ciples are threatened by an individual's total passionate involve-
> ment in a dyadic romance. (Regis 1995:143)

Self-directed courtship behavior appears most commonly where
autonomous mate selection is combined with romantic love as a valid
rationale for marriage (Pasternak, Ember, and Ember 1997:151).
While romantic love is probably universal, it is not always a legitimate
reason for marriage. In cultures where people live in nuclear families,
romantic love is more important; it is least important in cultures
where the husband and wife are in a relationship of *subsistence dependence* (p. 153). Subsistence dependence means that the two are dependent on each other and are also part of a larger kinship group with a
stake in their success. Romantic love could destabilize a marriage because two people are likely to be more committed to each other than to
the group, as the Fulbe fear. On the other hand, romantic love would
provide the glue for a couple remaining together in the absence of subsistence dependence or membership in a larger cooperative kin group.
This would be more likely the case in Western nations, such as the

United States. In the United States, in the late 1800s, the ideal of *companionate* marriage began to find fertile ground. This idea promotes marriage as a partnership where emotional and sexual intimacy is shared between equal partners and where the larger family demands on a couple are reduced in strength.

Suzanne Frayser (1985:249) finds that 86 percent of 59 societies select mates primarily on the basis of kinship, 8.5 percent on the basis of status, 3.4 percent on the basis of locality, and 2 percent on the basis of age. She cautions, however, that these figures are based on explicit, normative statements, and that reality is likely to reveal the picture to be more complicated. Nonetheless, kin group demands clearly play a predominant role in marriage choices across cultures. In spite of their premarital sexual activity Canela girls who lose their virginity to an adolescent boy may be taking their first step toward marriage (Crocker and Crocker 1994:155). Other steps toward marriage are marked by the ceremonial purchase of a husband by the bride's extended kin, the bride's winning of a ceremonial belt in ceremonies that include sequential sex, and the painting of the belt, especially by female in-laws (p. 156). When the time comes to marry, uncles lecture the bride and groom on marriage responsibilities and then leave them alone to have sex often (p. 156).

Sexual compatibility can play a powerful role in courtship, and some of the sexual permissiveness that so intrigues Westerners might be, in some cultures, better thought of as a selection process that will eventually lead to a more compatible and stable relationship. But it would be a mistake to consider courtship in permissive cultures to be merely a matter of sexual bonding. For example, in her study of romantic passion among Mangaians, Helen Harris reports that: "For Mangaians the courtship process was and remains a time not just for experimenting with physical intimacy, which as I have noted, eventually occurs for most people, but for establishing a close emotional relationship as well" (1995:110). Further, she observes in response to Marshall's earlier claim that sex occurs with almost every meeting during courtship, that "[c]ontrary to Marshall's contentions, courtships can remain chaste for weeks or months, and emotional intimacy may precede sexual involvement" (p. 111). Developing the intimacy of romantic passion requires giving the other person physical and emotional access to one's inner self (p. 111). Harris seeks to undermine the stereotype that sex is mere idle sport among Mangaians, which would play into the stereotype of primitive sexuality as being prone to unbridled and unfeeling sex. Malinowski ([1929]1987:242) points out that courtship and marriage among Trobrianders is also based on personality and character, not just physical compatibility. Whatever easy sexual trysts they might have when younger, Trobrianders mature into having more stable relationships that extend much beyond sexual exchange.

INCEST TABOOS

The incest taboo forbidding marriage and sexual relations between close relatives is a nearly universal prohibition. This is a simple statement that hides a multitude of problems, as evidenced by the following:

> Virtually all societies have customs restricting sex and marriage with people who are too closely related. We call such rules *incest taboos*. But precisely what sorts of people are "too closely related"? Would sex between a woman and her stepfather involve too close a relationship even though they are not related by blood? Further, what particular acts shall we consider incestuous? Apart from sexual intercourse, should we include acts that in themselves cannot lead to pregnancy, like fondling, genital manipulation, oral sex, perhaps even sleeping in the same bed? As a matter of fact, folk concepts display considerable variation from society to society in terms of which relatives (and other people) are too close for sex. (Pasternak, Ember, and Ember 1997:103–4)

The above passage raises two key questions: what constitutes "close" and what constitutes "sex" in relation to the incest restriction? As suggested above, these questions will be answered differently in different societies. As Burton Pasternak and his associates further note, marriage implies sex, but sex does not imply marriage, and thus we should distinguish between incest as a prohibition against sex and as a prohibition against marriage in order not to confuse issues (p. 103).

There is no single incest taboo, but a variety of taboos restricting sex and/or marriage among people who are related to each other to varying degrees. They operate most strongly against sex and marriage among members of the immediate family, that is, parents, children and siblings. The notable exceptions to this rule are the royal families of ancient Egypt, Hawaii, and Peru (Inca), who permitted sibling incest because they were untouchable by mere mortals and had no other way of continuing their line of descent. However, everyone else but the ruling family was under the rule of incest in the immediate family.

Why this universal prohibition? Theories about why there is an incest restriction cover biological, cultural, and psychological disciplines. Its widespread presence suggests an underlying genetic program, but it is clear that the incest taboo is often enough broken, thus weakening this argument. The problem of variable cultural definitions of incest further undermines genetic influence. Neither of these issues, however, necessarily precludes locating an ultimate genetic cause. In the end, however, the reason for their existence might be as simple as the two mentioned at the beginning of this chapter: the potential of sex to produce disharmony and its capacity to be attached to other institutions.

The idea that incest taboos exist because of the inevitable and deleterious genetic effect of inbreeding is a common one. It is premised on the assumption that somehow human groups with no scientific knowledge of genetics can nevertheless recognize birth defects and other anomalies as being caused, directly or indirectly, by incestuous sex and marriage. It might be possible for them to make this connection, however, by observing and remembering over generations that such anomalies appear more often than not among close relationships. Recognizing such a pattern does not mean it has to be attributed to genetic cause, but that it is perhaps caused instead by angry ancestors, or by sorcerers. We can make predictions without understanding the cause. Inbreeding may carry the potential for a high frequency of birth defects, but not necessarily depending on the frequency of anomalous genes in the gene pool in the first place.

Freud, Oedipus, and the Primal Horde

In developing his understanding of the incest taboo, Sigmund Freud turned a moral play into a psychodrama, and cultural evolution into fantasy. He offered a two-part explanation, one anchored in the psychology of childhood development and the other in speculative history. He modeled the Oedipus complex after the Greek myth of Oedipus who in ignorance married his mother but blinded himself in punishment when he discovered the truth of his incestuous relationship. Freud's Oedipus complex focuses on a primary frustration experienced by young males who come to realize that they must give up the nurturing attentions (feeding, bathing, comforting) of their mother. The mother in this theory is cast as the provider of pleasure to the infant, who, as he matures, wishes to continue his pleasurable existence. But a powerful father stands between him and his mother as a competitor for her affection. Somewhere around the ages of six or seven the Oedipus conflict is "resolved" when the boy makes the decision to give up his close attachment to his mother to seek other females. There is, however, no final resolution of the conflict, and the boy remains ambivalent toward his mother. This ambivalence, Freud argued, is the source of taboos against the object of ambivalence, the mother.

As noted in the opening chapter in this text, Malinowski took issue with Freud's claim that the Oedipus complex is universal. Freud worked with upper-middle-class clients in a patrilineal and patriarchal society, while Malinowski worked with Trobrianders who were a matrilineal, but not matriarchal, society where the mother's brother, not the father, is the authority figure. In this setting, boys have a warm, noncompetitive relationship with their father, but a tense one with their senior, maternal uncle. Malinowski reasoned, therefore, that conflict in the family had more to do with issues of power and authority than with sex. He believed further that incest taboos have more to do with role confusion that threaten to destabilize the family than with covert sexual desires between son and mother.

In his *Totem and Taboo* (1913) Freud speculates about how the incest taboo originally came about in a *primal horde* scenario. Freud sought to bridge the gap between his clinical practice and the taboos of native peoples by drawing a parallel between the emotional ambivalence of the neurotics he treated in clinical practice and what he saw as emotional ambivalence reflected in the taboos of native peoples. In making this identification of similarities between European neurotics and native peoples he set the basis for the claim that the incest taboo is not only universal but is universal for the same reason. He thus suggested that the incest taboo originated in the evolution of culture. Freud speculated that at some early point in human prehistory a primal horde existed under the control of a domineering and violent father who excluded his sons from sexual access to the women of the group, including mothers and sisters, and kept them for himself. Eventually, the frustrated sons rallied together, killed the father, and gained access to the women. Afterward they felt remorse for what they had done, and out of this remorse and respect for their father they gave up the women and created the incest taboo. Freud admitted that no such group was known, nor has one since been discovered, but asked that it be considered hypothetical. Experts today give the primal horde scenario no serious consideration.

Even if we find the Oedipus complex to be an untenable theory, we cannot so easily dismiss the fact that male identity and gender relations are often enough problematic and may be traceable in part to customs that accentuate a "natural" conflict among father, mother, and son (see Pasternak, Ember, and Ember 1997 for a review of explanations). In some cultures, for example the Sambia, men are fearful of sex with women and a good measure of sexual antagonism exists; some investigators have considered these practices as "exaggerated Oedipus" activities. These family dynamics might then generate various taboos against the sources of sexual ambivalence. Although Malinowski was himself ambivalent about whether he had really refuted the universality of the Oedipus complex, his analysis suggests that we may find different kinds of conflicts in different family systems and cultural settings.

Too Close for Comfort

Edward Westermarck (1922) proposed an "aversion theory" to explain incest taboos. He suggested that siblings who are raised together develop an aversion to physical intimacy with each other. In such circumstances there would likely be weak incest taboos because there would be no emergence of strong desires that would require strong taboos to counteract them. When, however, siblings are not raised in close contact, strong desires will more likely surface, requiring equally strong taboos to constrain them. Melford Spiro (1958) tested this idea in his study of the Israeli frontier communities known as *kibbutzim*. In these communities, children of both sexes were raised in large child-care centers for most of their pre-adult lives, but did not marry among themselves because they presumably were averse to having intimate relations with each other. Arthur Wolf (1970) studied families in northern Taiwan, where two forms of marriage exist: *major* and *minor*. Major marriages join partners who have not lived together as children, while minor marriages join partners who have. The potential bride in the minor marriage enters into the family as an adopted child, and thus the bride and groom live in the same house until marriage. Minor marriages exhibit a greater tendency toward conflict and fewer children because the husband and wife are not particularly interested in each other sexually. The aversion between husband and wife appears to be a result of growing up together. The evidence in recent studies is that Westermarck might have a point, but the evidence is generally inconclusive (Pasternak, Ember, and Ember 1997:110–18).

Marry or Die

Perhaps the most widely accepted theory on incest taboos today is Edward B. Tylor's (1871) "alliance" theory, which is summarized in his phrase, "marry out or be killed out." For Tylor, incest taboos are primarily ways of encouraging young men to look elsewhere for their marriage partners. By marrying outside a defined range of people, one can create strategic alliances with other groups for mutual cooperation and protection. However, marriage alliances are not always very effective. Nonetheless, in combination with the wish to avoid disruption in the family, requiring marriage outside the group gains explanatory strength. Many cultures feature rules of mate selection that can be classified as *exogamous* (outside a defined group), or *endogamous* (inside a defined group). The marriage rules work in conjunction with incest taboos because marriage implies sex.

Forbidden Unions

How "close" one can marry is defined in various ways. For example, many societies do not permit marriage with any cousin, but others permit marriage with some cousins. In some cultures, one can marry, from a male point of view, father's sister's daughter, and mother's brother's daughter—both are *cross-cousins*. They are called cross-cousins because the available daughters belong to a different-sexed sibling of the parents and thus belong to another male group or patrilineage. By the same rule, father's brother's daughter and mother's sister's daughter are off limits because the brother is obviously the same sex as the father on one side, and the sister is the same as the mother on the other side; both daughters are—*parallel cousins,* and most often the son cannot marry them on the grounds of incest. George Murdoch (1949) discovered in a cross-cultural survey that 57 percent of societies sampled disapprove of first-cousin marriage, as is true of the United States, while 43 percent do approve, but usually distinguish between the two types of cousins, parallel and cross.

Gregersen (1996:143–44) lists additional incestuous relationships. Muslim cultures define a "milk incest," in which those who have been breast fed by the same woman are forbidden to marry even if they are otherwise unrelated. "Spiritual incest" applies the incest rule to marriage between godparent and godchild in Catholic South America. Korea is well known for its "name incest" prohibition. A very large percentage of the country's population is divided up among only four or five family names, making much of the population at any one time off-limits for mate selection because of name sharing. No matter how distantly related, a Park cannot marry a Park, a Lee marry a Lee, or a Kim marry a Kim. To do so would commit incest. This law was changed in the 1990s.

Father–daughter incest is the most commonly *reported* violation of the incest taboo, both cross-culturally and in the United States. Mother and son incest appears to be more rare, but also may be underreported. Sibling incest may be more common than both, but underreported and usually more innocent. Sibling incest most commonly takes the form of sexual exploration without penetration among sexually immature children. As Pasternak, Ember, and Ember suggested earlier, such rudimentary sexual adventures may or may not be defined as sex. They might just be considered as play and viewed with varying degrees of tolerance and amusement. Father–daughter incest in the United States is often precipitated by a combination of factors including stress, a dominant and authoritative father and subordinate wife, and role confusion (Sirles and Franke 1989).

MARRIAGE

To define marriage in universally accurate terms is probably a fruitless enterprise. However carefully worded, definitions never quite cover all of the types of marriage that have been found cross-culturally and throughout history. Most definitions center on *sexual access, social legitimacy of offspring,* and *economic cooperation.* These components of marriage do in fact occur together widely, but not always. Rather than endlessly revising definitions, Pasternak, Ember, and Ember (1997:77–102) suggest that more to the point is the fact that most humans most of the time are engaged in a *stable, mated* relationship, regardless of how it might be defined. Even after death or divorce, most people enter a new stable, mated relationship.

Except for some rare forms of marriage, the ones that cause definitional problems, the overwhelming majority of marriages fall into one of three categories. Pasternak, et al. (1997:86, after Murdoch 1967) find that 83 percent of societies permit *polygynous* marriage (having more than one wife), 16 percent are *monogamous* (one spouse), and .05 percent are *polyandrous* (more than one husband). Where societies permit polygyny, most marriages are not actually polygynous because polygyny requires wealth and because it would take a tremendous sex ratio imbalance for all marriages to be polygynous. On the other hand, having multiple wives may actually produce wealth through their cooperative efforts. The available female population can be supplemented by raiding other groups for women, but then the raiding group subjects itself to retaliation and the loss of its own women.

In polygynous marriages men provide sexual service to multiple wives on a rotating basis. A man is expected to treat all of his wives the same, although in practice there are inevitable departures from the ideal, and jealousy, sexual and otherwise, can and does surface to create conflict among cowives. A man who already has two or more wives will often acquire an additional one purely out of romantic attachment. In this case, the young bride may arouse the jealousy and anger of her cowives because she may receive more gifts and more attention than others. It is possible that polygyny may exist partially to provide husbands with acceptable sex outlets when one wife is pregnant, but it probably has more to do with an expression of male power, wealth, and prestige. Marriage customs function to control sex indirectly through their ties with other aspects of culture that reinforce their hold over sex.

It would be difficult to overstate the importance of marriage in most societies where it is the premier gateway to adult social legitimacy. "One might forgo many cultural forms in Gabra life and still be a Gabra in good standing; marriage, however, was not one of them. . . . A basic assumption was that all persons eventually marry. That someone would never marry was unthinkable, absurd" (Wood 1999:126). As noted elsewhere, marriage forms relationships and changes statuses. John Wood sums up his observation of a number of marriages in Gabra (East Africa) society.

> Marriage, as we shall see, represents a series of significant changes
> in attachments and separations between individuals. The bride
> parts with her family and joins another, while the groom leaves be-
> hind his bachelorhood to become a responsible elder and eventually
> a father. The bride's and groom's families form an alliance: each
> gives and receives livestock, so herds mingle. In-laws observe rela-

tional avoidances, which simultaneously separate and call attention to their new and enduring intimacy. The ceremonies serve to
spell out and rehearse these new relations. (1999:128)

Wood's observations show how transformative marriage can be.

Still other forms of marriage exist. The Nuer of East Africa practiced same-sex marriage (Evans-Pritchard 1951). If a man has two
daughters and thus no male heirs, a daughter could marry another
woman (about 3 percent of the marriages). This is a symbolic arrangement only, not sexual. The female "husband" (who is sometimes
already married to a man) does not have sex with her "wife," but
when the wife bears children after mating with males, the female
husband becomes responsible for the offspring that result from such
matings. The female husband then can no longer have sex with her
male husband, although she can with other males. The purpose of
this arrangement is to continue the male line of inheritance that was
jeopardized by having no male heirs. This is another exotic practice
that makes sense more to us when we see it in the context of that
patrilineal culture. As we saw earlier, another African group, the
Zande, practice legal male–male marriage where warriors have "boy-
girls" who do domestic chores and have sex with the older men. The
men who took boys as wives were part of a bachelor category associated with the military (Murray and Roscoe 1998). In some African societies, young boys were taken as boy-wives involuntarily in a tradition of arranged marriages, where neither men, women, nor young
boys have many choices (p. xviii). Same-sex marriage is illegal in the
United States, except during a short time in Hawaii before its law
was reversed by the U. S. Supreme Court.

REPRODUCTION

Biological reproduction is the same for all humans, but we experience it differently in different places and times. We need to be aware
that *sexual reproduction* is a term that covers a number of elements. It
"refers to the physiology of human reproduction processes, including
menstruation, coitus, conception, gestation, frequency, parturition, infertility, abortion, and menopause" (Browner and Sargent 1996:220).
These elements of reproduction are shaped and toned by cultural beliefs and practices consistent with broader cultural contours as in the
examples above. As Carole Browner and Carolyn Sargent put it, "the
way a society structures human reproductive behavior inevitably
draws on and reflects that society's core values and structural principles" so that human reproduction is a social activity as much as it is a
biological one (p. 219). Even more specifically, the cultural molding of
human reproduction would include[2]

beliefs and practices surrounding menstruation; proscription on circumstances under which pregnancy may occur and who may legitimately reproduce; the prenatal and post partum practices that mothers-to-be and their significant others observe; the management of labor, the circumstances under which interventions occur, and the form such interventions may take; and comparative study of the significance of menopause. (Browner and Sargent 1996:219)

Female circumcision and infibulation attest to the extraordinarily high value that some cultures place on female virginity. While these practices are enmeshed in religious beliefs and folk medicine about the health and fertility of women, it is clear that their most important function is to establish control over female sexuality and reproductive function. These severe practices are not just random and disconnected customs but are very much an integral part of the political and economic system in which they are practiced. These communities stand in sharp contrast to the Canela where pre- and extramarital sex are encouraged and virginity is not an issue. Where one culture carefully guards sexual access to a woman, the other encourages sexual access within limits. These fundamentally different approaches fashion two contrasting constructions of sexuality; they represent quite different solutions to the problem of fitting human reproduction into their way of life.

Cultures form different schemas of how the invisible process of biological conception takes place. Some groups believe that the neonate is formed by the combination of women's blood and men's semen, both very visible signs of sexual identity that issue from genitals. A common schema in the Amazon Basin is that a healthy baby is produced by repeated additions of semen to the infant in the womb so that conception is not a onetime event but an ongoing building project. Malinowski (1929) claimed, with some evidence, that the Trobrianders believed that sexual intercourse had no necessary relationship to conception and that spirit agencies were responsible. As a result, the Trobrianders received some notoriety as a people who did not know that sexual intercourse is connected to reproduction. Yet in his special foreword (1987:ix) to the 1932 edition he explained that this "ignorance of paternity" was more complicated than such a simple statement suggested, although he took responsibility for the confusion.

The importance of controlling reproduction for political and economic reasons is underscored by a common form of wealth transfer between two parties known as *bride wealth*. This transaction establishes rights and obligations between the families of the groom and bride. The husband's relatives settle on a price, for example the number of cows, with the bride's family as compensation for the loss of her services. In some societies where the woman is of lower status than her husband, her family might have to provide a *dowry* to the groom's family as an encouragement to marry.

Westerners who assume that bride wealth is simply about selling women for profit are being ethnocentric. They see what appears to be a simple economic transaction where a woman is purchased as property, when actually the emphasis is more on setting up rights and obligations between the two parties than it is on purchasing a woman. It is true that these marriages are not based on romantic passion, but a woman's feelings, if strongly expressed, are sometimes taken into consideration. Yet, it is also true that women often have little choice. If a woman maintains the support of her own family, she may be able to counteract in some measure any unsatisfactory treatment by her husband. If the bride's treatment by her in-laws is truly unsatisfactory, her family can in some situations ask for penalties, call for the punishment of her husband by his own kinsmen, or request her return. In-laws do not usually want a divorce because they would lose a woman's services and suffer some damage to their reputation as well as having to return all or part of the marriage payment. Although bride wealth is only one of several kinds of marriage transactions, and each functions somewhat differently in different places, they all fulfill important social and economic roles (see Pasternak, Ember, and Ember 1997:156–58).

Children become subjects of economic decision making in a variety of family systems. Cross-culturally, marriages produce varying numbers of offspring in response to local economic circumstances. People frequently seem to make a cost/benefit analysis, consciously or unconsciously, about the desirable number of children they want. When families see a benefit in fewer children, they are more likely to value a smaller family. Most families in the United States see little reason to have many children because of the enormous expense they incur and because their labor is not needed in today's high-tech homes. Where they are seen as a benefit, for example in the families who operated large farms in the United States in the 1800s, families will be larger.

Family size can be controlled by a number of means in addition to contraception. *Infanticide* is one common technique of population control in some cultures (Frayser 1985:300). Most infanticide is performed for reasons such as a multiple birth or gender. Where males are valued, female infants are put to death. Extending breast feeding for several years is another method of birth control because women are less fertile when lactating. Some cultures follow a *post partum taboo* on sex between spouses for a period up to several years. Nations periodically become concerned over population increase or decline and set policies that reward or punish couples for having too few or too many children.

We have seen that many cultures connect children, resources, marriage, and sex in a strategic economic and political complex. The complex bears the potential to resolve issues of legitimacy, to exert control over sexual access, to maintain group integrity, and to reduce a source of conflict. But social and cultural conditions are subject to change as they did in the United States when the country's population shifted from predominantly rural to urban in the early twentieth century. The birthrate has continued to decline, more women than ever work outside the home, more unmarried couples are living together, modern sexual technology has advanced markedly, adoption rates are up, and same-sex partnerships are increasing. Marriage, romance, and reproduction are becoming disconnected. These changes occur as values and morality change, perhaps even driven to a degree by the political and economic changes themselves. These changes are beginning to take place in other cultures around the world as well.

EXTRAMARITAL SEX

As Frayser observes (1985:323–38), restrictions on premarital and extramarital sex really focus attention on the reproductive function of sexual access and should not be seen as simple moral restrictions. *A group's intensity of commitment to marriage and its restrictions tends to be reflected in the degree to which celebrations such as bride price and ritual are elaborated* (p. 328). In such cases, infertility and extramarital sex are common reasons for dissolving a marriage. Societies with less commitment to a marriage (hunters and gathers, for example) show less elaboration. A middle group between the extremes of commitment displays a greater variation. Frayser finds that there are more societies that allow premarital coitus for one or both sexes than those who do not. When there are restrictions, they are more likely to apply to extramarital than premarital relationships. More societies allow premarital sex for one or both sexes than those who do not. More societies permit men to have both premarital and extramarital sex than permit women to do either—the "double standard."

Generally, women face greater restrictions than men, who are almost always allowed more sexual latitude. Clearly, women are the principal targets of sexual prohibition. In a survey of 141 cultures, 36 percent required females to be virgins at marriage; 34 percent approved of premarital sex; and 29 percent permitted premarital sex when practiced discreetly (Broude and Green 1976). These figures indicate that nearly two-thirds of cultures permit premarital sex.

Although extramarital sex is generally not the stated norm cross-culturally, it commonly occurs. Men usually enjoy a much wider latitude in extramarital sex than women (Broude and Green 1976, 1980). Sexual adventure is punished harshly in some cultures and accepted in others as a fact of life contrary to stated norms. Discreet sexual affairs that do not draw the public attention are likely to be ignored. In some societies, like the Mehinaku, sexual trysts take on the quality of a game regardless of public values to the contrary. The Canela encourage extramarital sex because of their belief that the proper growth of the fetus depends on additional contributions of semen from worthy males, for example, good hunters (Crocker and Crocker 1994:83).

The West generally defines adultery as sex with anyone other than one's spouse. As we have come to expect, this definition encounters difficulties when applied cross-culturally. Fisher (1992:78) notes that the Lozi of Africa do not associate intercourse and adultery with each other at all; for example, accompanying a married woman down a path is considered adulterous. Wood reports for the Gabra of East Africa that "sexual contact between a man and an unmarried woman . . . resulted in banishment. It was considered the worst crime in Gabra society, easily comparable to murder. And banishment was the most severe punishment. The two were cast out, *chabani*, broken from the whole" (1999:126). The woman would be sent to a neighboring community where unmarried women were sexually active, and the man would remain in the community but forbidden ever to participate in Gabra rituals. The man had committed a crime against property and had to pay a fine to the woman's family. Once married, however, women had considerable sexual freedom, and once circumcised, men were expected to pursue sexual affairs with married women. The Gabra, then, reverse our expectation that marriage is supposed to restrict sexual access rather than free it from constraint.

Clearly, we are not by nature monogamous creatures. Fisher (1992:90–91) suggests that there may have been evolutionary reasons for this. From a female perspective, she argues, adultery may have had some adaptive functions, mainly that it provides a woman with supplementary sustenance from lovers and some insurance against the loss of her husband. Lovers often give gifts to each other, usually male to female, and in some cultures men exchange meat for sex (Siskind 1973). A lover might marry a widow. On the other hand, such adventures can easily lead to jealousy and violence, which might impair a group's chances for survival.

About 80 percent of Americans disapprove of extramarital sex (Michael et al. 1994:84). Robert Michael and his associates note that Americans believe that their sexual lives are, and should be, governed by internal factors, but in actuality seem to be more influenced by social surroundings (p. 16). Thus their sexual decisions are affected by social circumstances such as class, religion, and education. In a questionnaire response, more than 80 percent of women and 65 to 85 percent men of all ages report complete fidelity (p. 105), which Heidenry (1997:412) calls the conformist view of sex in America that is not to be uncritically accepted.

DESCENT

Marriage creates a relationship through *affinity*, often presented graphically as a horizontal tie among couples of the same generation. Descent creates blood, or *consanguineal*, relationships that tie past, present, and future generations to each other in a lineage. As a son or daughter, we have blood relationships with both parents, but under descent rules one relationship counts as more important than the other. In cultures where descent plays an important organizing role, one line, for example traced through the father, his father, and his father, might be the most important one for economic and political reasons and takes precedence over the line traced through the mother and her mother. The overwhelming majority of societies, as noted earlier, emphasize the male line; they stress patrilineal relationships. In such a system the mother belongs to a different male line from the father's; children belong to the lineage of their father. Other societies like the Trobrianders are matrilineal (children belong to the mother's lineage). Both systems come under the heading of *unilineal* descent which simply means that descent is traced through one line. A member of a descent group in traditional societies can trace his or her actual relationship to a founding ancestor. Your membership in a descent group is an example of an ascribed status; you were born into it through no choice of your own. In addition to these systems, there is an *ambilineal* system where an individual makes a *choice* of which line (male or female) to emphasize, and *bilateral*, where both sides are acceptable.

Clans are larger kin units that organize lineages under them. One of the characteristics of a clan is that the founding ancestor, unlike the lineage founder, is unknown. The reason the founder is unknown is because memory of his identity is lost in the haze of far distant generations, and therefore he is simply *stipulated*. Often the ancestor is an animal or other creature in the environment whose habits are well known, or he is a combination human/animal whose origin, and therefore the clan's birth, is explained in terms of adventures in the mythic past. A clan forms a core of cooperating kinsmen who settle disputes, regulate land use, organize for warfare, and arrange marriages. They define who are legitimate marriage candidates, and those with whom marriage would be incestuous.

DIVORCE

Helen Fisher's (1992) excursion into the biological basis of love, sex, and marriage is one based on discovering how our evolutionary history continues to influence our behavior today. Recognizing that much of our behavior beneath the cultural clothing that makes us seem so diverse is consistent across cultures, she finds that divorce peaks among most cultures at about the fourth year of marriage. This length of time corresponds with the time it takes for one's initial biochemical infatuation with their lover or spouse to wane. The fact that she is able to demonstrate that this phenomenon is widely experienced throughout the world leads her to conclude that we are biogenetically programmed for infatuation, followed by deinfatuation. With the waning of the biochemical rush of love, divorce is a likely, but not necessary, result. She is quick to add that divorce is not inevitable, because we have other needs that can sustain long-term relationships. Indeed, intimacy and partnership can biochemically produce calming emotions. Infatuation, she reasons, may be a biochemically driven device in humans that evolved to allow males to spread more genes among more partners rather than commit to just one in an extended relationship. This advantage, however, could be offset by the male's greater parental investment in fewer offspring.

Marriage involves certain understandings and expectations at both individual and group levels that if not fulfilled threaten to a dissolve the union. Cultures vary in the ease with which they permit divorce. Frayser (1985:260) discovered that 62 percent of the 45 societies she surveyed make it difficult for one or both partners to secure a divorce; 38 percent allow one or both partners to dissolve a marriage easily. The Gabra have no formal mechanisms for divorce, although elders may try to talk a couple out of separating (Wood 1999:128). Social pressures can be quite heavily weighed against divorce, especially if marriage is seen as joining two groups in the manner mentioned by Wood. The payment of "childwealth" in Igbo (Nigeria, West Africa) society is an example of marriage as a union of two groups rather than two individuals. It also illustrates how children become economic factors when the union is dissolved.

> For a divorce to be total the woman's family must return the marriage payment to the husband; any child the woman might subsequently have would then no longer be claimed by her husband. For this reason the marriage payment has sometimes been referred to as childwealth—that is, the child belongs to whoever has made the payment; otherwise it belongs to the child's mother's patrilineage. (Amadiume 1987:71)

Cross-culturally, women most commonly divorce their husbands because of (in order of most- to least-frequent reason) incompatibility, failure to meet economic responsibilities, or physical violence, while men cite reproductive problems (assumes infertility of the wife), incompatibility, and illicit sex (Frayser 1985:258). Laura Betzig (1989) surveyed 160 societies and found in contrast to Frayser that adultery is the most common cause of divorce. Illicit sex and infertility as causes of divorce reflect the importance that some groups place on controlling the woman's reproductive capacity and reflect how sex, marriage, and reproduction are interwoven.

In contrast, the history of sexuality in the United States records a continuing tendency to divide sex, reproduction, and marriage from each other. Unlike lineage and descent systems, marriages are seen as a union of individuals and thus easier to form and easier to dissolve. Physical violence, not infertility or illicit sex, is a frequent cause of divorce in the United States. The ease of obtaining a divorce, its current lack of stigma, and the increasing economic freedom of women are among the ingredients contributing to the high divorce rate. Divorce was at its highest in 1979 at 5.3 per thousand population, but has since declined to 4.2 per thousand population in 1997. In 1997 there were nearly one million divorces compared with 1,213,000 in 1981. The divorce rate hovers close to 50 percent (Laumann et al. 1994). Although North Americans tend to see marriage as a less permanent state than they did in the decades before the 1960s, in expectations of continuing passionate romance and intimacy, family role flexibility, and a cooperative, sharing enterprise, they also seem to be asking more of marriage than did prior generations.

SUMMARY

All cultures regulate sex in some manner, but principally through the incest taboo, marriage, and descent. Incest taboos are universal, but defined differently cross-culturally. Although universal, incest taboos are often broken, usually with consequences for one or both parties. Like other animals, we court potential mates, but specific practices vary widely and may include sexual intercourse during or at the end of the process.

In spite of some rare types of marriage formed under special circumstances, the overwhelming number of cultures either permit polygyny or require monogamy. In polygynous societies, most marriages are monogamous, while in monogamous societies, a pattern of repeated marriage and divorce suggests that *serial monogamy* might be a better term to describe the pattern of marital bonding. In cultures where families tightly control access to the reproductive capacity of women, premarital and extramarital sex may be forbidden and carry heavy penalties for violators. Cultures may present such controls as a matter of morality, but this rhetoric masks a deep concern over economic rights to women and their offspring. Many groups feature bride wealth as a way of reinforcing new relationships that marriage establishes between the families of the bride and groom.

In marriages based on romantic passion, divorce could be precipitated by the diminished brain receptors for feel-good biochemicals associated with love. On the other hand, long-term relationships also produce soothing chemicals. The fact that so many divorces cross-culturally are related to women's reproductive capacity highlights its economic and political importance. Such is not the case in the West where extended family systems and economic rights in children are not the norm.

CRITICAL INQUIRY

---

1. What are your expectations of marriage? Is extramarital sex ever acceptable? Is obtaining a divorce in the United States too easy? Explain your answer.

2. How would you describe courtship patterns among your own age group?

3. What sexual values and practices would you like to see changed in your country? What are the chances that would happen? Explain.

NOTES

---

[1] This view of love madness is not confined to the Fulbe but often is the case with Islamic-influenced cultures, which include the Fulbe.

[2] While it is beyond the scope of this text to explore each of these facets of reproduction in great detail, we should understand that a full appreciation of sexuality and reproduction in any culture would require a rather full-scale investigation of the schema employed by a culture to connect these elements with each other and to other institutions.

Chapter Six

Sexual Issues

The sexual issues we visit in this chapter—prostitution, pornography, sexual violence, and sexually transmitted diseases—have marked human life since ancient times. Their persistence tells us something fundamentally important about ourselves. Explanations of their timelessness range from sociobiological and socioeconomic causes to moral failure. One point is clear, however: these sexual issues are so widespread that they must be regarded as universal elements of human sexual potential. This chapter builds a better understanding of the conditions under which these human sexual realms are ignored, tolerated, encouraged, accepted, or prohibited. Setting these issues in their contexts and viewing them against a cross-cultural background will prove valuable. It must be remembered, however, that these are "issues" for some cultures and not for others. Some individuals may believe that they require remedies, others may not. Because they have been defined as issues in North America, Europe, and elsewhere, we address them here.

PROSTITUTION

References to prostitution appear early in ancient history (Bullough and Bullough 1978). In the Near East, the Code of Hammurabi (Babylon) in 1700 B.C. refers to beer houses that might have been houses of prostitution. Prostitution is known to have been common in the Near East and basically ignored by law (Gregersen 1996:152). As early as 650 B.C. China provided brothels for merchants. In India, the Kama Sutra discussed what a successful prostitute should do. The

Greeks operated state-run brothels in 594 B.C., supplied in part by Greek parents who sometimes sold daughters who had lost their virginity to houses of prostitution. The Romans registered prostitutes and manufactured special brothel coins. Generally, Europe regarded prostitution to be a necessary evil, so the periodic campaigns to eliminate it were followed by long periods of disregard. A number of African preliterate cultures in Nigeria, Algiers, and Egypt also had prostitutes (Gregersen 1996:154–55). In the seventeenth century, Japan featured one of the most famous "red-light" districts in the world, with some three thousand prostitutes working out of over one hundred houses. Japanese prostitutes often were young daughters sold to tea houses by poor parents.[1]

Various observers of prostitution have ascribed its persistence to male lust, moral defect, a way of preserving female virginity (among "respectable" women), and the marginality of women in capitalist society. Our purpose here, however, is not to develop a final explanation of prostitution (if that is even possible) but rather to assemble a more accurate picture of the circumstances of its occurrence and to question common understandings and definitions.

Our common understanding of prostitution encounters definitional difficulties cross-culturally. Usually, we define it as *selling sexual services indiscriminately for payment*. The seller provides the buyer with a service for a fee. The transaction implies neither intimacy nor a long-term relationship. Normally we think of prostitution in terms of brothels, streetwalkers, and callgirls. But prostitution is more complex than a simple fee for service transaction that is usually thought to characterizes these pursuits. This definition, for example, might not cover the temple prostitutes of India whose activities are sanctioned by their religion. Where would women in the harems of the Near East fit in this definition? Would the term apply appropriately to the exchange of meat for sex among hunters of the Amazon? How do we classify the short-lived marriages of wealthy Western men to beautiful young women with scarce economic means? What about concubines and mistresses? We might consider these cases to be exchanges of sex for consideration, that is, a return of something of value, yet they raise questions about how to classify interactions that are not always unidimensional. If there are components of social or religious sanction, affection, or varying degrees of coercion involved, how should these interactions be characterized and labeled?

These questions broach issues about how elastic we want to make the term *prostitute*—how wide a range of culturally nuanced sexual transactions do we include in its definition? We also quickly encounter the problem of how other cultures themselves classify various sexual liaisons. They might entertain different values as reflected in the fact that prostitution is not necessarily illegal or sinful in other places. What is true is that humans engage in a wide variety of sexual relationships under a wide variety of conditions, some of which are approved by society, some of which are not, and others of which are ignored. Rather than to argue definitional points here, we shall take the term as commonly understood in North America and Europe in order to clarify issues of larger concern to us.

Prostitution in North America

Prostitution became more salient in the United States in the 1700s with the burgeoning of urban life and maritime trade. The French and Indian War in the 1750s caused further changes in the organization of colonial life and indirectly stimulated the growth of prostitution. For example, rising levels of prostitution in the city were an early sign that the traditional community surveillance of sexual behavior was breaking down (D'Emilio and Freedman 1997:50). The emergence of a large number of single men in the late 1700s in large eastern cities and on the western frontier was another key factor in the growth of prostitution. Prostitutes in the United States at this time were almost exclusively poor white women, and some were undoubtedly alcoholics. Even in the South, few black women entered prostitution in this era. Against the assumed sexual purity of married women, prostitutes were regarded as "fallen" women.

The Civil War fostered additional prostitution as women gathered close to military camps in both the South and the North. The Union army on campaign in the South attracted numerous prostitutes as the Southern economy was collapsing. In the 1880s, immigrant women arrived regularly without sufficient economic resources to see them through the transition to life across the Atlantic, and many became prostitutes as a matter of survival. Meanwhile, on the West Coast, thousands of Asian women were imported as sexual slaves for both white and Asian men (p. 135). Many large cities developed substantial "red light" districts as urbanization continued into the twentieth century.

With the growth of cities and influx of immigrants from abroad, commercial sex became not just a growth industry but a key part of urban life, involving prostitutes, pornographers, and wealthy investors.

> In New York, from 1820 to 1920, sexual intercourse became an activity increasingly directed by economic and market forces. Prostitutes, together with abortionists, pornographers, distributors of contraceptive aids, and the organization of various leisure institutions in which they flourished, turned sexuality into something to be sold. Sex became a profit making venture.
>
> As a personal, intimate, and nonmarketable commodity, commercialized sex illustrated one significant conquest of the market in the nineteenth century. (Guilfoyle 1992:20)

New York was not the only eastern city experiencing the surge of commercial sex, but one of the most explosive. The visible arrival of sex in some quarters of the city provoked a vigorous response from the public health authorities. While middle-class sexuality had been changing in value and behavior, the public visibility of commercial sex seemed to exceed the limits of toleration.

In the early 1900s, a white slavery panic developed with "purity crusaders" searching the country for sexually enslaved white women, of whom there were many fewer than supposed in the minds of the crusaders (Guilfoyle 1992:208). The crusade was largely alarmist hype, but the crusaders also targeted immigrant women as lowering the standards of white morality. In World War I, prostitutes again gathered in force near military bases, but authorities established a five-mile "purity" zone around the camps. The regulation, however, was unevenly enforced. More important the authorities chose to emphasize chastity instead of prevention. The result was an outbreak of venereal disease. In the 1920s red light districts, where most houses of prostitution were located, were closed by authorities, displacing prostitutes to the streets or to become callgirls. The continued attack on the morality of immigrants assumed racial tones as it was directed mostly at southern and eastern European women who immigrated in poverty (Guilfoyle 1992).

Although the rising incidence of venereal disease further motivated attempts to control prostitution, urban growth and industrial expansion in the twentieth century continued to generate circumstances where prostitution could flourish: a number of single men moved to cities to seek employment, the dense population in urban areas made it easy for married men to encounter women outside of the family, and community surveillance could be avoided in bustling, crowded urban areas. These conditions, with immigration, produced a large body of women who were poor and unattached. Many had drug and alcohol problems. All were candidates for prostitution. Black women now increasingly entered prostitution in the North.

Today the United States criminalizes prostitution in all states, except for a few counties in Nevada. The police make about 90,000 arrests each year, about 10 percent of which are clients. As was suggested earlier, the term prostitution covers a variety of exchanges and in fact may conceal the real complexities of sex work. Normally, we think of streetwalkers, brothels, and callgirls, but what about lap dancers or phone sex workers? Callgirls differ from streetwalkers in that they are better paid to provide emotional exchanges along with sex and are involved in the so-called commercialization of intimacy (Lever and Dolnick 2000). This difference reflects the fact that men seek prostitutes for a variety of reasons, not simply for quick sexual release (Monto 2000).

Most women in the United States enter prostitution for negative reasons, such as prior sexual abuse, poor education, poverty, alcoholism, addictions, and low self-esteem. On the other hand, highly publicized cases like the Heidi Fleiss case (prostitution for male stars) in Hollywood and the madame in *The Happy Hooker* indicate that some women might enjoy the life and the money. For whatever reason they became prostitutes, some women feel themselves to be in control of their sex work. Margo St. James founded COYOTE (call off your old tired ethics) in 1975 as a prostitution rights group dedicated to normalizing and decriminalizing prostitution. However, radical feminists see prostitution as sexual slavery driven by the priority we give to men's sexual needs.

Thai Sex Tourism

Prostitution in Thailand illustrates the effect poverty can have on young women and represents a case of the exotic sold as the erotic (Bishop and Robinson 1998). It is sex tourism blatantly sold as such, and marketed principally to Western men who arrange to visit Thailand for easy and inexpensive sex in a tropical setting, with young, attractive, and compliant young women. The sex tourism industry involves tour operators, airlines, and the powers behind the sex trade. It is an integral part of the global sex industry. Regular tourist advertisements feature ancient ruins, a tropical environment, and a woman, usually smiling. Images of women easily outdistance those of men in the travel literature on Thailand (Bishop and Robinson 1998:711–73). Although tourism is internationally pushed by various international agencies as a way of breaking down cultural stereotypes and building cross-cultural understanding, most travel brochures for Southeast Asia, regardless of the country they tout, play up those images of exotic women and places that appeal to Westerners and therefore play to stereotypes.

Sex tourism is a large and integral part of the Thai economy, contributing as much as four billion dollars per year (Bishop and Robinson 1998:9). Prostitution is technically illegal, but laws geared to national development and tourism in general have clouded the issue. Prostitution gained a firm hold in Thailand during the war in Vietnam, when the country agreed to permit large numbers of United States servicemen to take their rest and relaxation leaves there. In the late 1980s to 1990s, prostitution grew by half. Today foreign men visit alone or through organized sex tours. Eighty-nine percent of the tourists who come to Bangkok, the capital, are men (p. 67). But, to understand better what Thai sex tourism is about, we need to go beyond the statistics, to the full context of its origin and its continuation:

> For anyone seeking to understand the economic underpinnings of the
> sex industry, the first requisite would be a description of the rural

economy, the migration of village youth to swell the supply of cheap, unskilled urban labor, the development of mass international tourism, and the ways these intersect. (Bishop and Robinson 1998:94)

The large number of prostitutes required to meet the huge demand for them is recruited from impoverished villages by promises of work. Families gladly let their daughters leave because they see that other families who sent their daughters to Bangkok live in better houses, have more consumer goods, and consume a better diet. Daughters do not tell their families what they are really doing in the city. The task of earning an income for the family then falls heavily on the daughters, who are working for their family and not for themselves. They could work in the sweatshops of Bangkok up to sixteen hours per day, but they would earn less and have no opportunity for the "big score," meeting someone who would support them financially. If they are working in the international sex trade, they also have nice clothing, some cosmetic surgery should it be required, and regular physical examinations.

Houses serving white men (who are known as *farangs*) are centered in three famous red-light areas: Patpong, Soi Cowboy, and Nanda. Other places cater to Japanese, Chinese, Indians, and Arabs. Men meet prostitutes in bars and take them for a one-night stand. Often, these short meetings are extended over time as the men find someone who suits them on a more regular basis. Many establish longer-term relationships with prostitutes spanning weeks, months, or years. Some fall in love and marry. Some of these unions last for years, but most fall apart quickly.

Sex is important in Thai culture, but it is not considered the essence of life or person. In Buddhist thought, sex is of the body and of the world both of which followers view as transient and relatively unimportant. Detachment from the world as it is merits more attention than the messy details of everyday life. Sexual misconduct by women is thought to be a result of some failure in their prior life. This perspective may allow women to separate their selves (identity and emotions) from their bodies and their sexual activities. They might therefore escape some of the psychological damage reported for prostitutes in the West, but it is not clear that they escape completely unaffected.

Thai prostitution illustrates the point made earlier about reinforcing cultural stereotypes rather than changing them. Western men are attracted by compliant Thai prostitutes who stand in sharp contrast to demanding and insensitive (as the men see it) Western prostitutes. Men say that the Thai women are more responsive to them emotionally than are Western women, and that such intimacy is hard to find among women of any kind in their own countries. The intimacy the men feel, however, is mostly illusionary on their part. Much anecdotal evidence suggests that the men themselves are largely lonely men who have failed at relationships in their home countries (Seabrook

1996; Bishop and Robinson 1998). Whether or not this is in the end an accurate psychological assessment, it is clear that the same sexual exchange has a different cultural meaning to each party involved.

The men take the women's emotional labor in being compliant participants as natural and sincere—an essence of their identity. They delude themselves into thinking that they have established a relationship only to be surprised when the women suddenly disappear. The women do not want to be thought of as victims because they feel that they have some control over relationships. They are actually looking for the big score by convincing a man to hand over a large sum of money, for example, to help out in a manufactured family crisis. Alternatively, they can save smaller amounts of cash over a longer period of time. Many women plan to set up their own business in Bangkok or in their home village. Men on the other hand feel that they were led on by the apparent sincerity of the women and by their own infatuation, only to be progressively relieved of their money. Many men leave Thailand realizing that they never were in charge.

Prostitution in the United States and in Thailand is driven to a high degree by the poverty and powerlessness of women and by a body of men looking for quick and unencumbered sex. Thailand, however, is well situated in the international sex tourism industry, and the exotic, youthful appearance and compliant presentations of the prostitutes in Bangkok make them attractive to outsiders. If the Thai case is any indication, sex tourism does not break down cultural stereotypes, but rather reinforces them.

Phone Sex

When we fall in love, become infatuated, chemicals such as dopamine are released in our brain making us feel better, even elated. Love junkies are those who repeatedly fall in love, and perhaps become addicted to this biochemical rush and continually seek it. With deinfatuation, the receptors in the brain have become dulled to the effect, and the infatuation ends. *Aphrodisiacs* are extrabody substances used as sexual stimulants throughout the world. While there are many aphrodisiacs on the market, only a few actually work. Fantasy, on the other hand, is one of the most powerful and effective stimulants to sexual desire, and we carry it in our head at all times. In her study of the phone sex industry, Amy Flowers (1998) maintains that her subject really is not the phone sex business but the *disembodiment of intimacy*. Human interaction is mediated by technology that frees people of the "constraints of physical disability, stigma, and stereotype" (p. 2). In the phone sex industry, fantasy and reality are confused. The training of phone sex workers promotes the exploitive skills of deception, role playing, and manipulation. The point is to get the caller more involved so that he (the overwhelming number of callers are males) stays on the phone for a long time, accumulating minutes for which he must pay. Flowers suggests that phone sex prostitutes (sex workers' self-label) indulge in a form of *emotional labor* (see also Hochschild 1983). They are selling to their callers their own ability to engage them in emotional/sexual exchanges. Although workers try to maintain distance between themselves and their callers, almost all workers at one time or another are caught believing that the callers are being forthright about themselves rather than also being manipulative.

Phone sex workers must struggle with impression management on the phone and self-esteem in private. One way they attempt to maintain self-esteem is by thinking of their jobs in purely economic terms and by separating themselves from other kinds of sex workers. In a recent study, Grant Rich and Kathleen Guidroz (2000:40) found that phone workers took the job because it paid reasonably well and they needed money. The workers are not entirely immune to the effects of their work on their own sexual lives; they tend to become more inventive sexually and embrace a wider range of sexual experiences in their own relationships. Although workers reported that their own sex lives improved, they had more negative feelings toward men because of callers' interest in violent sex, mutilation, and sex with children. They usually felt that they could talk easily about sex over the telephone, but in some operations, they are allowed to turn down calls to which they object. Rich and Guidroz conclude that the results of their study should challenge the notion of sex theorists that "sex work is inherently oppressive and demeaning to the workers" (p. 48).

PORNOGRAPHY AND EROTICA

Depictions of erotic human sexual expression span the full length of history. Middle- and upper-class living rooms of ancient Pompeii displayed sexually explicit murals, while the TV sets of modern North America receive both soft- and hard-core porn. Although not present in all cultures, depicting human sexuality has been a constant in human behavior throughout the millennia. What varies is the degree of public acceptance. Sexually explicit graphic images or literature can be ignored, discouraged, encouraged, or made criminal at various times in the same culture. Today's contemporary college textbooks on human sexuality, with photographs and illustrations of sexual anatomy and techniques of coition, could have been labeled obscene and their authors jailed, even in the twentieth century.

Pornography has Greek roots that mean to write about harlots. Its contemporary meaning in the United States relates to obscene and objectionable material. The range of erotic and sexually explicit material that the term covers shrinks or expands according to who uses it. Thus the term can cover birth control information, European classical nude paintings, Greek statues, Mochica pots, or the latest XXX movie. Photographs of bare-breasted white women might be pornographic, but those of native women might be acceptable. Because of the difficulty of fashioning a precise definition, the United States Supreme Court has based its considerations of obscenity relative to local community standards of what is acceptable. This stance is counterbalanced by the First Amendment on freedom of speech. A softer version of pornography, referred to as *erotica*, has become more acceptable to a wider viewing public.

Until just before the Civil War, Americans had access to only a small number of reprints of erotic classics from Europe, like *Fanny Hill*. In fact, an Irish surgeon, William Haynes, used the profits from his publication of this erotic classic to launch a series of cheap erotic novels beginning with *Confessions of a Lady's Waiting Maid* (1848). The market for erotic material expanded significantly with the Civil War because men were separated from their families for long periods of time. Erotic photographs became available to Civil War soldiers for the first time. While these developments began to raise some alarm among the public, Americans up to the time of the Civil War seemed more content to focus on "individual purification" through self-control rather than public regulation (D'Emilio and Freedman 1997:57). Prior to the Civil War, only four states had enacted obscenity laws.

After the Civil War, the YMCA started a countermovement against the public expression of sexuality. The organization decried what it saw as the lack of adult supervision over young men in cities who visited theaters and were free to encounter prostitutes on the street. One YMCA member launched a wide and vigorous campaign against lewd and obscene literature. Anthony Comstock's national crusade ended successfully in 1873, when the Comstock Act was passed by Congress. A broadly conceived piece of legislation, it covered, in addition to explicit sexual material, medical advice on contraception and sex education. At the same time, the Women's Christian Temperance Union (WCTU) and other purity movements gained momentum. The Comstock Act remained in effect well into the twentieth century. Under its rule, some classic books were prevented from entering the United States, notably, James Joyce's *Ulysses* and D. H. Lawrence's *Lady Chatterly's Lover*. These were serious literary works by widely esteemed authors that were banned for being obscene.

The 1960s and 1970s witnessed a number of challenges to institutional authority in the United States The Civil Rights movement, protests against our involvement in Vietnam, and the women's liberation movement all sought fundamental reform and redress. The women's movement was joined by the Gay Liberation Organization.

All attacked some key assumptions and values that previously had been thought to be widely shared by most Americans. This development was paralleled by the publication of numerous books promoting sexual satisfaction for both men and women, such as Alex Comfort's *The Joy of Sex*, which first appeared in local bookstores across the country in the early 1970s.

Also by the 1970s, movie houses on Main Street America screened "X-rated" movies such as *Deep Throat*, *The Devil in Miss Jones*, and *Debbie Does Dallas*. This trend, however, was short-lived as communities soon reasserted themselves and displaced these films to marginal theaters or banned them outright. The introduction and popularity of the video films quickly replaced the movie theater as a source of sexually explicit images. Videos could be bought or rented and viewed in the privacy of one's home.

A conservative backlash against the sex business began with the election of Ronald Reagan as president in 1984. Cultural conservatives guided national discontent toward reform by launching campaigns against pornography and questioning sex education. In 1985, Attorney General Edwin Meese formed a commission, staffed for the most part with political conservatives, to study the effects of pornography, especially with respect to sexual violence. It concluded that pornography leads to violence and is therefore a threat to social order. The study is largely discredited today. However, one of the persisting questions in the study of pornography is whether or not it is linked to sexual violence against women. Unfortunately, such studies tend to ignore the general presence of violence in the United States even in the absence of pornography. Moreover, there are many forms of pornography having nothing to do with violence and perhaps would better be labeled as erotica. Indeed, one point that clouds this issue is that the general public, who might in fact occasionally view some erotic magazines or videotapes, is perhaps unaware of how violent some sexually explicit films can be.

The feminist movement itself split at one point over the issue of violence and pornography. One section led by Andrea Dworkin (1985) and Catherine MacKinnon (1985) argued that all pornography commits violence against women by viewing women as sexual objects to be used as men wish. Another section headed by feminists such as Gayle Rubin (1984) and Carol Vance (1984), who, while aware and disapproving of the clear sexual violence and degradation of women in some pornography, were nevertheless concerned with freedom of speech issues and with the implicit notion that women are not sexual creatures interested in sexual activity.

There is no clear evidence that pornography leads to sexual violence. As in the profiles of people who are prone to commit rape (discussed further in the next section), however, there are those viewers of violent pornography who are already predisposed to violence and who are probably also the most likely to act violently. In this case, viewing violent material involving women might trigger action, but the cause of sexual violence might lie elsewhere in a person's psyche. Some laboratory studies have suggested that viewing pornography desensitizes the viewer for a time afterward. Does desensitization lead to violent behavior? There is no evidence that it does. There are several problems with these studies.

1. Many studies of the effects of pornography establish a correlation, for example, a rapist admits viewing violent pornography before acting. A correlation establishes an association between two variables, but one might not cause the other; they both might be caused by a third variable. The correlation might be coincidental and not be explainable at all.

2. Laboratory studies can be fruitful, but how well do they relate to real life? If a modest increase in desensitivity follows a viewing, does that predict a probable behavior in real life?

3. Pornography suffers from definitional problems, but other important definitions are involved in these studies. Definitions of obscenity, violence, and domination are part of research studies but are not as easily agreed on as one might think.

SEXUAL VIOLENCE

Sexual violence includes a wide variety of forced or coerced sexual acts from parental–child incest and child molestation to war rape and wife rape. It is a term that on the one hand calls attention to a greater variety of offensive acts than we would normally think of when defining rape, but on the other hand can be so inclusive as to risk confusion. For example, men often rape women in wartime; sometimes rape is sanctioned as a reward for soldiers for a successful campaign and/or is used as a terrorist tactic (Hayden 2000).

In the United States, *rape is the forced sexual penetration of genital, anal, or oral body openings* (statutes vary in different states). In *statutory rape*, the age of the victim is below a certain legal age, normally from fourteen to eighteen years, while the "rapist" is adult. These sexual encounters might on the surface be consensual rather than forced sex, but that fact is legally irrelevant, because the victim is legally too young to give consent. Rape is now often further subdivided into *date rape* (involving a degree of coercion between two people who know each other) and *stranger rape*. These are all punishable offenses in the United States. Like pornography and prostitution, rape considered cross-culturally encompasses a wider or narrower range of behaviors than in the United States or in Western nations in general.

In some cultures rape is an appropriate punishment for a woman who has violated a custom. In some Native American communities, rape was a traditional way of punishing a woman for adultery. Some Amazonian groups store sacred trumpets in the men's house, which they bring out at certain times for important ceremonies. If women should even inadvertently view the trumpets they are liable to be subjected to gang rape. How often these sanctions are actually imposed is unclear. In still other cultures marital rape would be legally impossible because marriage gives men complete control over their wives. In some cultures, a woman abandoned by her husband is vulnerable to rape without the rapist fearing retribution from her husband or kinsmen. In most cultures, rape, although perhaps quite rare, does occur but is not accepted and the offender is treated severely.

Why do men rape? In the United States, some feminists, such as Susan Brownmiller (1975), Catherine MacKinnon (1985), and Andrea Dworkin (1985) contend that sexual violence, male dominance, and female degradation are inherent even in consensual heterosexual intercourse. MacKinnon observes that without violence, there is no sexual arousal in men. Other feminists such as Gayle Rubin (1984) and Carole Vance (1984) argue to the contrary. The former group argued that pornography leads to rape, while the latter argued that pornography challenged the traditional definition of female sexuality. Some evolutionary psychologists take the position that rape is an alternative mating strategy developed in our evolutionary past by less successful males (Thornhill and Palmer 1999), but there is no way to know this for sure. Cross-cultural studies by Sanday (1981) and Broude and Green (1976) make a distinction between rape-free and rape-prone cultures. Rape-prone cultures are also cultures whose values and social structure reflect the dominance of men, while rape-free cultures do not. Whether or not rape is absolutely absent in rape-free cultures or is a product of evolutionary processes that make it universal, the two cross-cultural studies make it clear that cultural conditions are important in heightening or dampening the incidence of rape.

The United States has the highest incidence of rape in the Western world—about one-half million reported cases per year. Over 90 percent of the victims are female, and 99 percent of the perpetrators are male. Almost all rapes are committed by people who are the same race as their victims (88 percent). Studies of rapists in the United States reveal no single pattern in terms of psychological profile or sociological background. They may or may not be psychologically disturbed or have criminal records. Women are raped almost exclusively by someone they know or to whom they are related. Only about 4 or 5 percent of rapes are stranger-initiated. Because rape is primarily between those who know each other, issues such as sexual coercion, rape myths, and sexual scripts emerge in importance. The common idea among men, that a woman who says no is really saying yes and just putting up token resistance, is both a myth and a sexual script—a cognitive schema that defines the situation and relationship. Men in the United States are in fact held responsible for acts that are construed as rape at the point at which a woman says no, regardless of what has happened previously between the two people. Myths and scripts are no excuse for rape. Scripts and myths are tied, in this case, to traditional role definitions that cast men as aggressive and women as submissive. Rape survivors are more likely to tell a relative or friend of the assault than to contact the police. Survivors can suffer long-term physical injuries (including contracting HIV) and mental trauma (Rathus, Nevid, Fichner-Rathus 2000:566–68).

The new phenomenon in rape in the past decade is the use of drugs on unsuspecting women, usually by slipping a substance into their drink. Rohypnol, commonly known as *rufies*, is a sedative hypnotic that produces an amnesia effect. Not only is the person rendered helpless, but she remembers little or nothing of the episode. It takes about an hour to reach its peak in the bloodstream, but it is detectable in urine for four days or so afterward. Another drug gaining in use is GHB, which takes effect almost instantly. It also produces memory loss. A 1996 federal law adds twenty years to the sentence of a man convicted when such drugs are involved. As a consequence of the use of these drugs, especially on college campuses, women must be wary of everyone around them and, particularly, they must keep an eye on their drinks.

SEXUALLY TRANSMITTED DISEASES

Contrary to popular opinion, Europeans contracted syphilis as a result of contact with Native Americans, not the reverse (Baker and Armelagos 1988). Nevertheless, the early European explorers, merchants, and military personnel played important roles in spreading STDs around the world as a result of their voyages. In the year 2000, five hundred years after Columbus's initial voyage to the New World, there were about 340 million cases of curable STDs (excludes AIDS) worldwide (WHO.int). The United States has the highest incidence of STDs in the developed world. More than 65 million people in the United States are living with an incurable STD; each year, 15 million more people become infected with STDs (CDC.gov).

The widespread prevalence of STDs in the world, however, has been eclipsed in the global consciousness by the HIV/AIDS (human immunodeficiency virus/acquired immunodeficiency virus) pandemic. HIV/AIDS is now the leading killer among all infectious diseases and the fourth among all causes of death. The World Health Organization estimated in 1998 that some 47 million people had been infected in the previous fifteen years; the Centers for Disease Control (CDC) in Atlanta estimates that there were about three million new cases reported in 2000. About 95 percent of new cases, and 95 percent of deaths, occur in developing countries. Most severely affected are young people and, increasingly, women. The incidence of HIV infections is on the rise among younger age groups where adolescents are more experimental and less knowledgeable about sexual risk. Young women are more susceptible to infection because the vaginal lining is thinner and more easily torn or abraded. In the United States, the cumulative number of cases reported to the CDC as of the year 2000 is 753,907, of which males total 620,189, females 124,911, and children under the age of age thirteen 8,804.[2] The most vulnerable years are from about 20 to 45. The cumulative death toll from AIDS in the United States is nearing half a million.

HIV is the underlying cause of AIDS. The HIV virus eventually undermines the immune system to such an extent that it becomes ineffective against a variety of pathogens and renders it vulnerable to various diseases. At this point the infected person has AIDS. HIV is transmitted through contact with the body fluids of an infected person. It is not curable at present, but is manageable (in developed countries) at great cost and with persistent effort. Although the biological impact of AIDS on an individual is severe enough, it also has a tremendous negative impact on communities in third- and fourth-world countries as people lose friends and relatives and families lose their breadwinners, mothers, and sometimes their children.

> Nearly 70 percent of the world's HIV-positive individuals live in Africa. Masses of orphans have been created. About one-third of all children borne by infected women will have AIDS themselves. Kin networks that would ordinarily care for the orphans and the sick children may be structurally too weak to do so because so many family members have died off. Once-productive villages are no longer self-sufficient; labor shortages can lead to famine, increasing vulnerability to HIV infection. (Loustaunau and Sobo 1997:167)

The biological component of AIDS is essentially connected with the social and cultural in both its patterns of transmission, its effect, and attempts to prevent or treat it.

> Perhaps more than any other disease in modern history, AIDS demonstrates the complex interactions between a disease agent and human behavior within varying ecological contexts. More pointedly, the AIDS pandemic underlines the need to understand ecological context as social, political, and economic—that is cultural as well as biological. (Brown, Inhorn, and Smith 1996:208)

This view mirrors our own insistence on defining the context in which sexuality is conceptualized and enacted. Without a solid grounding in the social and cultural context, no prevention program can hope to be effective. The following sections explore this relationship as they address transmission patterns, folk theory, sexual choices, and prevention programs.

STD and HIV Transmission

HIV transmission follows different patterns of infection in different places. In the United States, HIV was initially transmitted through homosexual partners and needle-sharing drug users, while in Africa it is transmitted primarily through sexual contract by heterosexual partners. The spread of HIV in Africa is closely associated with modernization, especially increasing geographical mobility such as among long-distance truck drivers, migrant workers, military personnel, traders, salesmen, and prostitutes. These groups characteristically have multiple sex partners and carry infection back home to their wives and girlfriends. This pattern is extended when infected mothers in turn give birth to infected children.

Studying patterns of transmission necessitates identifying high-risk groups, but doing so often requires the researcher to challenge stereotypes and misconceptions that outsiders often have about such groups. Because they service multiple partners, often without condoms, prostitutes usually fall into the high-risk group. Yet, the term *prostitute* actually indiscriminately covers a wide range of sexual realities as suggested earlier in this chapter. It is easy for Westerners, for example, to picture a woman walking her designated area of a city block or occupying a cheap hotel room while consumed by drugs and isolated from a larger network of friends and kin. But this is not the case depicted earlier for Thailand, where prostitution does not stem from instability and is a temporary phase of life, with prostitutes often returning to their homes to live (although they still are at risk as Thailand has an increasing incidence of HIV infection). Prostitutes in Africa also are not usually isolated from other facets of life.

A simplistic understanding of prostitution can have a misleading influence on prevention planning. As Brown, Inhorn, and Smith (1996:211) observe, women in commercial sex are often thought to be simply "reservoirs of HIV infection," rather than links in social networks of noncommercial relationships spanning urban and rural settings and encompassing families and friends. Nor do simple messages about condom use targeted at prostitutes match the reality of their more complex human relationships. Advocating the use of condoms among commercial sex workers may have some beneficial result, but this message runs up against the fact that refusing to have sex with a man who won't use a condom may guarantee a loss of badly needed income. In addition, a significant other who demands that a man from home use a condom is often seen as untrusting.

Folk Theory

Sub-Sahara Africa suffers from a stereotype (with the unwitting aid of anthropologists) that it has no medical system and recognizes only personalistic (rather than natural) causes of disease such as witchcraft and sorcery. "The popular stereotype of African indigenous medicine is of magic, witchcraft, sorcery, and spirit possession, set against a background of throbbing drums" (Green 1999:11). As a consequence, international health authorities usually (until lately) ignore actual indigenous beliefs and tend to blame program failures on the stereotype. This attitude has begun to change due in large part to anthropological voices stressing the need to understand local knowledge and behavior in order to secure effective local participation.

The core task is to discover how the target population conceptualizes the etiology, treatment, and prevention of specific diseases. Lately, basic terminology with respect to sexually transmitted diseases has changed. Sexually transmitted disease, STD, is the terminology of Western biomedicine. The local cultural terminology is referred to as sexually transmitted illness, STI; it is the *folk theory* of illness (Green 1999:135 after Hahn 1984). Sexually transmitted illness is sometimes confused with another biomedical term, sexually transmitted infection, which is used by public health authorities (p. 135). Edward Green found that, contrary to the stereotype, "Africa's most serious diseases tend to be interpreted within a framework that is essentially naturalistic and impersonal" (p. 12). STDs are included in this category.

Green (1999) refers to the local understanding that is based on natural causes as ICT or indigenous contagion theory (making it a form of STI). He argues that throughout Africa, many healers conceptualize the same naturalistic infections as does the Western biomedical model. For example, in Mozambique, he found that people stress naturalistic agents and pollution as causes of STDs (p. 171). Treating a disease caused by pollution (through breaking a taboo or mixing bodily fluids) requires avoidance behavior. Thus, the advice of prevention programs to avoid situations where body fluids are exchanged makes perfect sense to local healers. Similarly, many healers emphasize marital fidelity and reducing the number of sex partners to combat AIDS (p. 177), a strategy consistent with outside programs of behavior modification. Healers recognize fully that sex outside of marriage increases the risk of contracting an STD for whatever reason. Green is convinced that much more can be done with behavior modification and that planners rely too heavily on remedies that focus on condoms. In Zambia, a long period of condom promotion has yielded little result, while in Uganda there has been a decline of disease in part because of behavioral changes (p. 174; see also Brown, Inhorn and Smith 1996:195, 210).

Sexual Choices

Identifying high-risk groups and clarifying sexual choices are two key areas of investigation in prevention studies. Brown, Inhorn, and Smith note that we must critically examine high-risk groups with respect to "the dynamics of sexual decision making and networking" (p. 210) in order to formulate effective policy. Here are a few common factors in sexual decision making in Africa and elsewhere.

1. *Economic survival.* Commercial sex workers are often reluctant to turn away men who refuse to use a condom because of the workers' dire need for income. Women sometimes use a strategy known as lateral fertility to spread economic risk by securing potential support from among multiple sex partners. That is, they try to guarantee continuing income by servicing a core of steady customers.

2. *Women lack empowerment.* Women often do not feel empowered to require their husband to use a condom.

3. *Specific cultural beliefs.* Mixing bodily fluids may be a valued way of sharing among groups. Bodily fluids may be closely connected with fertility or the proper growth of the fetus by repeated contributions of semen by the husband and/or other men. Fertility is frequently seen as an essential part of a woman's identity and condom use might be seen as a threat to that identity.

4. *Interpretation of condom use.* A man may interpret a woman's insistence on the use of a condom as a lack of trust; either partner may view the use of a condom as an admission that the other already has an STD.

5. *Erroneous belief.* Men entertain risky beliefs that sex is safer with younger, rural women and with friends who are less likely to have AIDS or other STDs.

These "choices" not to use condoms are not characteristic of Africa alone. Sobo (1995:25–50) finds that disadvantaged women in the United States tend to believe that the use of condoms sends a negative signal about the state of a relationship. Some feel more secure having sex with someone they know, and many feel that they can trust their husbands to honor the marriage vow. They consider fertility and sexuality as fundamental elements of their personal worth.

Prevention Programs

Condoms usually present a huge expense to Africans as their cost can constitute a sizable portion of an individual's income. There are many brands available, but some are of poor quality, and condoms can deteriorate in the African heat and humidity. Green (1999:173) reports widespread skepticism about condom use among healers. They say that condoms often burst, and that they do not cover the entire shaft of the penis anyway, so that any lesion, for example chancroid (leads to an ulcerative condition common in Africa), can transmit HIV. This is yet another reason why Green (pp. 176–77) believes that planners focus too much on condoms and not enough on behavior modification.

Green enlisted the aid of traditional healers in several prevention programs in Mozambique and Zambia. An important part of his work was based on his understanding of how the healers classify STDs, their transmission and treatment. Working on this project convinced him that healers recognized naturalistic causes and that this recognition could be a point of contact between them and outside health authorities operating in the context of Western biomedicine. In her study of unsafe sex behavior among disadvantaged women in Cleveland, Ohio, Elisa Sobo (1995:25–26) emphasizes that women have the basic facts about HIV risks, but that these facts do not necessarily replace other "facts" about HIV transmission that they know. Her message is, like Green's, that simple education programs may be a start toward prevention, but they cannot guarantee genuine behavioral change unless planners address STD issues as they are understood by local men and women.

SUMMARY

Whether or not a culture considers the subjects of this chapter to be "issues," they are nevertheless persistent sexual behaviors or the results of those behaviors. We must therefore regard them as part of the human sexual potential and identify the circumstances under which they occur. In doing so, we need to remember that human sexuality is malleable and easily attached to wider cultural concerns and institutions. As we examine these issues, we again encounter labeling problems that threaten to throw us off our analytical track. We tend to see "prostitutes" as solitary workers devoid of a network of friends and family, which is a conception that does not hold in reality. Even the relationship between a prostitute and her client is often more complex than commonly understood. In the United States, most of the women who work as prostitutes do so because of negative personal circumstances, but Thai prostitutes are more often working for their family. Thai prostitution represents a case of the exotic sold as the erotic and does more to reinforce Western stereotypes than it does change them. Sex workers in the phone sex industry sometimes refer to themselves as prostitutes. They trade in fantasy and deceptive manipulation in an effort to extend the length of the call for financial gain. But the deception often threatens to overcome them and affect their self-concept.

Sexually explicit videos also trade in erotic fantasy. Pornography and erotica are big business, and videotape and cable television allow middle-class Americans to view them in the privacy of their own home. The relationship between watching pornography and committing sexual violence is unclear, but it appears that a relationship is most likely present in those who are already prone to sexual violence. In the United States acquaintance rape is by far the most common type. Cross-cultural data suggest that a general climate of violence heightens the probability of sexual violence.

We find the overwhelming number of new HIV/AIDS cases in the developing countries, especially in Africa. Regardless of location, effective programs of prevention and aid need to be designed on the basis of a thorough understanding of the cultural characteristics of the target population.

CRITICAL INQUIRY

---

1. Is prostitution inevitable? What would you do about it, if anything? Is you position moral, practical, other?

2. To women: You decide to go to an off-campus party in a revealing dress. Why?
   To men: You see a woman in a revealing dress at an off-campus party. What are you thinking? The woman is later raped. What is your response?

3. Which do you worry more about, acquiring HIV/AIDS or acquiring other STDs? How do you resolve the issue of trust vs. contraception in a relationship?

NOTES

---

[1] In spite of their reputation in the West, Geishas are not prostitutes, but skilled in dancing and singing, they are educated and refined hosts. Although they may enter into discreet affairs with lovers, they do not sell sex.

[2] Although the number of cases reported totals 753,904, CDC reports 753,907 as the total.

Chapter Seven

The Future of Sex

What will our sexual experiences be like in the future? What consequences will we suffer, what benefits will we enjoy? What currently developing conditions might affect future patterns of sex? Predicting the course of sexuality into the near and moderately near future is risky, as is any prognostication about the future because we do not know what unexpected developments might occur. Prediction usually involves a straight-line projection and tenuous assumptions about current conditions remaining constant, without all the unexpected and messy contingencies that might in fact appear. No one, for example, foresaw the appearance of AIDS and the toll it would take on human communities.

We should step into the future on the firm basis of the past. Understanding sexual issues and sexual diversity can best be accomplished by placing them firmly in their cultural context and against their broad historical and cross-cultural background. By emphasizing this strategy we can avoid the deficiencies in knowledge and perspective that have plagued discussions of sexual issues in the past. This approach has the additional benefit of establishing our cultural and sexual commonality, from which point we can move with greater assurance into issues of human and sexual diversity. Given the complexity of human sexuality, this venture will continue to require interdisciplinary effort and multiple theoretic perspectives.

Human sexuality is shaped by the events and forces that impinge on other elements of culture as well. Sexuality does not exist in a vacuum but is entwined with other institutions, such as marriage and descent, and is subject to various economic and political forces. It is bound up with gender roles, social classes, and religion. Thus, it is more often the case that sexuality is indirectly influenced through these institutions than it is the direct recipient of attention, although the latter often seems to be the case.

Describing a sexual pattern, a normative picture of sexual practices and values, establishes a baseline from which to view sexual change and variance. Individual members of society, however, may live up to norms with varying degrees of success, for all humans probably entertain at least a few desires and fantasies for sexual experiences that fall outside the normative range. To harbor fantasies is not abnormal, but they may not be defined as normal in a given culture. Sex patterns change over time, leaving individuals to go along as best they can. Indeed, what is normative sex at one moment may become problematic at another. Individuals may not be certain what the accepted sex pattern is because it is in transition or is in a prolonged state of flux with competing patterns. This indeterminancy is characteristic of modernity.

Modernity is spreading throughout the world via international trade, travel, and the global media. Western cultures influence marriage, love, and sex around the world. Gender roles are changing, and young girls demand their piece of the modern world, while at the same time many remain embedded in traditional systems and roles (Inness 1998). Economies are changing with repercussions for courting, marriage, and sex. Contraception is making increasing inroads in other countries. One repercussion of change is that it fosters a continuing divorce of sex and reproduction from each other.

Anthony Giddens (1992) suggests that sexuality in the United States and England today is a struggle of the self to cope with modernity, that is, the constantly shifting, indeterminate understandings and expectations of modern life. Sex is cut loose from reproduction, but where do we go from there? The rise of romantic love and the subsequent release from reproductive responsibilities change the nature of relationships from those centered on family and reproduction to one based on intimacy, the *pure relationship* in Giddens's words (1992). He views this development as a revolutionary change in sexuality. The pure relationship is based on the qualities inherent in the persons involved rather than on group economic or political strategies. *Plastic sexuality* (in the sense that it is pliable) is characteristic of this relationship as sex becomes not a behavior but an essential expression of who you are, for example, bisexual, homosexual, or heterosexual. Intimacy combines sexual behavior with a wider range of emotional engagement between partners. He sees intimacy providing the potential for men and women to escape the "rule of the phallus" and for men to open up to talk. Opening to the other is a form of democracy. It is not the kind of intimacy that Western men seek from women in the Thai sex industry, that is intimacy on men's own traditional terms. He notes that men, like sex tourists, complain that modern women have lost their capacity for kindness and compromise.

Giddens further argues that men are dependent on women emotionally but are unable to handle this recognition well. Men are not incapable of romantic love, but they lack emotional autonomy. What is needed, he says, is confluent love where both partners open out to each other and democratize their love. But the word sexuality, which first appeared in the eighteenth century, has come to denote a political battleground (Giddens 1992:182), a power struggle between men and women and between institutions and self. Whether or not his assessment is ultimately correct, he raises some interesting questions about intimacy, sex, and person in the twenty-first century. These questions have cross-cultural implications as other countries see their economies change, traditional family systems strained, and a continuing separation of sex and reproduction. Will they redefine the purpose of sex?

Virtual sex, phone sex, and cybersex raise issues about the disembodiment of intimacy. Dial up your personal fantasy on demand or chat with others who share your fantasy. But what is intimate about a chat room where individuals can easily misrepresent who they are and who you probably will never embrace? In a time of increased sexual freedom and possibility, we now profess a concern with intimacy. Is it really intimacy we are interested in or is it that old wish to control free and easy sex that seems ready to spin out of control? Yet, given human capacity for attaching emotions and meanings to sexual acts, should we avoid addressing questions of intimacy and similar inquiries into the full complexity of sexuality? In the near future we are likely to continue seeing the existence of alternative and competing sexualities (sexual pluralism) cross-culturally, and even within cultures, and to continue efforts to match our values to changing sexual technologies. Heidenry (1997) claims that the sexual revolution is not over, that it will continue to reverberate throughout the world.

But where do we go from there?

Bibliography

Ainsworth, M. D. 1964. Patterns of Attachment Behavior Shown by the Infant in Interaction with His Mother. *Merril-Palmer Quarterly* 10:51–53.

Altman, Dennis. 2001. *Global Sex.* Chicago: University of Chicago Press.

Amadiume, Ifi. 1987. *Male Daughters, Female Husbands: Gender and Sex in an African Society.* New York: Zed Books (Palgrave).

Baker, Brenda J. and George J. Armelagos. 1988. The Origin and Antiquity of Syphilis. *Current Anthropology* 29(5): 737.

Bardaglio, Peter W. 1999. "Shameful Matches": The Regulation of Interracial Sex and Marriage in the South before 1900. In *Sex, Race, Love: Crossing Boundaries in North American History,* Martha Hodes (ed.), pp. 112–38. New York: New York University Press.

Barker-Benfield, G. J. 1975. *Horrors of the Half-Known Life.* New York: Harper and Row.

Bell, Jim. 1995. Notions of Love and Romance among the Taita of Kenya. In *Romantic Passion: A Universal Experience,* William Jankowiak (ed.), pp. 152–65. New York: Columbia University Press.

Betzig, Laura. 1989. Causes of Conjugal Dissolution: A Cross-Cultural Study. *Current Anthropology* 30:654–76.

Bishop, Ryan and Lillian S. Robinson. 1998. *Night Market: Sexual Cultures and the Thai Economic Miracle.* New York: Routledge.

Blackwood, Evelyn and Saskia E. Wieringa. 1999. Introduction. In *Female Desires: Same-sex Relations and Transgender Practices Across Cultures,* Evelyn Blackwood and Saskia E. Wieringa (eds.), pp. 1–38. New York: Columbia University Press.

Block, Sharon. 1999. Lines of Color, Sex, and Service: Comparative Sexual Coercion in Early America. In *Sex, Race, Love: Crossing Boundaries in North American History,* Martha Hodes (ed.), pp. 141–63. New York: New York University Press.

Bowlby, R. 1969. *Attachment and Loss.* New York: Basis Books.

Brettell, Caroline B. and Carolyn Sargent. 2001. *Gender in Cross-Cultural Perspective,* 3rd ed. Upper Saddle River, NJ: Prentice Hall.

133

Broude, Gwen J. and Sara J. Greene. 1976. Cross-Cultural Codes on Twenty Sexual Attitudes and Practices. *Ethnology* 15:409–30.

———. 1980. Cross-Cultural Patterning of Some Sexual Attitudes and Practices. *Behavior, Science Research* 15:181–218.

Brown, Donald E. 1991. *Human Universals.* New York: McGraw-Hill.

Brown, Helen Gurley. 1962. *Sex and the Single Girl.* New York: Bernard Geiss.

Brown, Peter J., Marcia Inhorn, and Daniel J. Smith. 1996. Disease, Ecology, and Human Behavior. In *Medical Anthropology: Contemporary Theory and Method*, Carolyn F. Sargent and Thomas M. Johnson (eds.), pp. 183–217. Westport, CT: Praeger.

Browner, Carole H. and Carolyn F. Sargent. 1996. Anthropology and Studies of Human Reproduction. In *Medical Anthropology: Contemporary Theory and Method*, Carolyn F. Sargent and Thomas M. Johnson (eds.), pp. 219–234. Westport, CT: Praeger.

Brownmiller, Susan. 1975. *Against Our Will: Men, Women and Rape.* New York: Simon and Schuster.

Buckley, Thomas and Alma Gottlieb, eds. 1988. *Blood Magic: The Anthropology of Menstruation.* Berkeley: University of California Press.

Bullough, Vern L. 1976. *Sexual Variance in Society and History.* Chicago: University of Chicago Press.

Bullough, Vern L. and Barbara Bullough 1978. *Prostitution: An Illustrated Social History.* New York: Crown.

Burton, John W. 2001. *Culture and the Human Body: An Anthropological Perspective.* Prospect Heights, IL: Waveland Press.

Buss, Donald. 1994. *The Evolution of Desire.* New York: Basic Books.

Carrier, Joseph M. and Stephen O. Murray. 1998. Woman-Woman Marriage in Africa. In *Boy-Wives and Female Husbands: Studies of African Homosexualities*, Stephen O. Murray and Will Roscoe (eds.). New York: St. Martins.

Caulfield, M. D. 1985. Sexuality in Human Evolution: What Is Natural Sex? *Feminist Studies* 11(2): 343–63.

CDC.gov. 2001. Centers for Disease Control, Atlanta.

Chomsky, Noam. 1957. *Syntactical Structures.* The Hague: Mouton.

Comfort, Alex, ed. 1972. *The Joy of Sex: A Gourmet Guide to Love Making.* New York: Simon and Schuster.

Crocker, William and Jean Crocker. 1994. *The Canela: Bonding Through Kinship, Ritual, and Sex.* New York: Holt, Rinehart, and Winston.

D'Emilio, John and Estelle B. Freedman. 1997. *Intimate Matters: A History of Sexuality in America*, 2nd ed. Chicago: University of Chicago Press.

Davis, Katherine B. 1929. *Factors in the Sex Life of Twenty-two Hundred Women.* New York: Harper and Row.

de Munck, Victor. 2000. *Culture, Self, and Meaning.* Prospect Heights, IL: Waveland Press.

Douglas, Mary. 1966. *Purity and Danger: An Analysis of Concepts of Pollution and Taboo.* New York: Putnam.

Dworkin, Andrea F. 1985. Against the Male Flood: Censorship, Pornography, and Equality. *Harvard Women's Law Journal* 8:1–29.

Eibl-Eibesfeldt, I. 1989. *Human Ethology.* New York: Aldine de Gruyter.

Ekman, Paul. 1973. *Darwin and Facial Expression.* New York: Academic Press.

Ellis, Havelock. 1933. *The Psychology of Sex.* New York: Random House.

Evans Pritchard, E. E. 1951. *Kinship and Marriage Among the Nuer.* Oxford: Clarendon Press.

Faery, Rebecca B. 1999. *Cartographies of Desire: Captivity, Race, and Sex: The Shaping of the American Nation.* Norman, OK: University of Oklahoma Press.

Ferraro, Gary. 2001. *Cultural Anthropology: An Applied Perspective.* Belmont, CA: Wadsworth.

Fisher, Helen. 1992. *Anatomy of Love: A Natural History of Mating, Marriage, and Why We Stray.* New York: Fawcett.

Flowers, Amy. 1998. *The Fantasy Factory: An Insider's View of the Phone Sex Industry.* Philadelphia: University of Pennsylvania Press.

Ford, Clelland S. and Frank A. Beach. 1951. *Patterns of Sexual Behavior.* New York: Ace.

Foucault, Michel. 1978. *The History of Sexuality: Vol. 1: An Introduction.* New York: Pantheon.

———. 1985. *The Use of Pleasure: The History of Sexuality: Vol. II.* New York: Pantheon.

———. 1986. *The Core of the Self: The History of Sexuality: Vol. III.* New York: Pantheon.

Frayser, Suzanne G. 1985. *Varieties of Sexual Experience: An Anthropological Perspective on Human Sexuality.* New Haven, CT: HRAF Press.

———. 1999. Human Sexuality: The Whole Is More than the Sum of Its Parts. In *Culture, Biology, and Sexuality,* David N. Suggs and Andrew W. Miracle (eds.), pp. 1–16. Athens: University of Georgia.

Freud, Sigmund. 1913. *Totem and Taboo.* New York: New Republic.

Giddens, Anthony. 1992. *The Transformation of Intimacy: Sexuality, Love, and Eroticism.* Stanford: Stanford University Press.

Gilmore, David D. 1990. *Mankind in the Making: Cultural Concepts of Masculinity.* New Haven: Yale University Press.

Givens, David B. 1983. *Love Signals: How to Attract a Mate.* New York: Crown.

Godbeer, Richard. 1999. Eroticizing the Middle Ground: Anglo-Saxon Relations Along the Eighteenth Century Frontier. In *Sex, Love, Race: Crossing Boundaries in North American History,* Martha Hodes (ed.), pp. 91–111. New York: New York University Press.

Goffman, Erving. 1959. *The Presentation of Self in Everyday Life.* Garden City, NY: Doubleday.

Gordon, Daniel. 1991. Female Circumcision in Egypt and Sudan: A Controversial Rite of Passage. *Medical Anthropology Quarterly* 5:3–14.

Green, Edward C. 1999. *Indigenous Theories of Contagious Disease.* Walnut Creek, CA: Altamira Press.

Gregersen, Edgar. 1996. *The World of Human Sexuality: Behavior, Customs, and Beliefs.* New York: Irvington Publishers.

Gregor, Thomas. 1977. *Mehinaku: The Drama of Daily Life in a Brazilian Indian Village.* Chicago: University of Chicago Press.

Gruenbaum, Ellen. 2001. The Movement Against Clitoridectomy and Infibulation in Sudan: Public Health Policy and the Women's Movement. In *Gender in Cross-Cultural Perspective,* 3rd ed., Caroline Brettell and Carolyn Sargent, (eds.), pp. 481–92. Upper Saddle River, NJ: Prentice Hall.

Guilfoyle, Timothy J. 1992. *City of Eros: New York City, Prostitution, and the Commercialization of Sex, 1790–1920.* New York: Norton.

Hahn, Robert A. 1984. Rethinking "Illness" and "Disease." *Contributions to Asian Studies* 18:513–22.

Harner, Michael. 1968. The Sound of Rushing Water. *Natural History* 77(6): 28–33.

Harris, Helen. 1995. Rethinking Heterosexual Relationships in Polynesia: A Case Study of Mangaia, Cook Island. In *Romantic Passion: A Universal Experience,* William Jankowiak (ed.), pp. 95–127. New York: Columbia University Press.

Hayden, Robert M. 2000. Rape and Rape Avoidance in Ethno-National Conflicts: Sexual Violence in Liminalized States. *American Anthropologist* 102(1): 27–41.

Heidenry, John. 1997. *What Wild Ecstasy: The Rise and Fall of the Sexual Revolution.* New York: Simon and Schuster.

Herdt, Gilbert. 1981. *Guardians of the Flutes: Idioms of Masculinity.* New York: McGraw-Hill.

———. 1987. *The Sambia: Ritual and Gender in New Guinea.* New York: Holt, Rinehart, and Winston.

Herskovits, Melville J. 1938. *Dahomey: An Ancient West African Kingdom.* New York: Augustine.

Hinton, Alexander L. 1999. Introduction: Developing a Biocultural Approach to the Emotions. In *Biocultural Approaches to Emotions,* Alexander L. Hinton ed., pp. 1–38. New York: Cambridge University Press.

Hite, Sheer. 1976. *The Hite Report.* New York: Macmillan.

Hochschild, Arlie Russell. 1983. *The Managed Heart: Commercialization of Human Feelings.* Berkeley: University of California Press.

Hodes, Martha ed. 1999. *Sex, Love, Race: Crossing Boundaries in North American History.* New York: New York University Press.

Inness, Sherrie A., ed. 1998. *Millennium Girls: Today's Girls Around the World.* New York: Rowman and Littlefield.

Irvine, Janice. 2000. Doing It with Words: Discourse and the Sex Education Culture Wars. *Critical Inquiry.* 27:58–76.

Jankowiak, William, ed. 1995. *Romantic Passion: A Universal Experience.* New York: Columbia University Press.

Johanson, Donald C. 1981. *Lucy: The Beginning of Humankind.* New York: Simon and Schuster.

Kendall. 1999. Women in Lesotho and the (Western) Construction of Homophobia. In *Female Desires: Same-sex Relations and Transgender Practices Across-cultures,* Evelyn Blackwood and Saskia Wieringa (eds), pp. 157–78. New York: Columbia University Press.

Kinsey, Alfred C., Wardell B. Pomeroy, Clyde E. Martin, and Paul H. Gebhard. 1948. *Sexual Behavior in the Human Male.* Philadelphia: Saunders.

———. 1953. *Sexual Behavior in the Human Female.* Philadelphia: Saunders.

Krafft-Ebing, Richard von. 1886. *Psychopathia Sexualis: Eine Klinisch-forensische Studie.* Stuttgart: F. Enke.

Kulick, Don and Maud Willson. 1995. *Taboo: Sex, Identity, and Erotic Subjectivity in Anthropological Fieldwork.* New York: Routledge.

Lauman, Edward O., John H. Gagnon, R. T. Michael, and S. Michaels. 1994. *The Social Organization of Sexuality: Sexual Practices in the United States.* Chicago: University of Chicago Press.

———. 1997. Circumcision in the United States: Prevalence, Prophylactic Effects and Sexual Practice. *Journal of the American Medical Association* 277:1052–1057.

Le Pichon, Yann. 1987. *Gauguin: Life, Art, Inspiration.* New York: Abrams.

Lever, Janet and Deanne Dolnick. 2000. Clients and Callgirls: Seeking Sex and Intimacy. In *Sex for Sale: Prostitution, Pornography and the Sex Industry*, Ronald Weitzer (ed.), pp. 85–100. New York: Routledge.

Lock, Margaret. 1993. Cultivating the Body: Anthropology and Epistemologies of Bodily Practice and Knowledge. *Annual Review of Anthropology* 22:133–55.

Loustaunau, Martha O. and Elisa J. Sobo. 1997. *The Cultural Context of Health, Illness, and Medicine.* Westport, CT: Bergin and Garvey.

Lutz, Catherine. 1988. *Unnatural Emotions: Everyday Sentiments on a Micronesian Atoll.* Chicago: University of Chicago Press.

MacKinnon, Catherine A. 1985. Pornography, Civil Rights, and Speech. *Harvard Civil Rights-Civil Liberties Law Review* 20:1–70.

Malinowski, Bronislaw. (1929)1987. *The Sexual Life of Savages in North-Western Melanesia.* Boston: Beacon Press.

Mandell, Daniel R. 1999. The Saga of Sara Muckamugg: Indian and African American Intermarriage in Colonial New England. In *Sex, Love, Race: Crossing the Boundaries in North American History*, Martha Hodes (ed.), pp. 72–90. New York: New York University Press.

Marshall, Donald. 1971. *Sexual Behavior on Mangaia In Human Sexual Behavior*, Donald Marshall and R. Suggs (eds.), pp. 103–162. New York: Basic Books.

Martin, Emily. 1987. *The Woman in the Body.* Boston: Beacon Press.

Masters, William H. and Virginia E. Johnson. 1966. *Human Sexual Response.* Boston: Little, Brown.

———. 1970. *Human Sexual Inadequacy.* Boston: Little, Brown.

———. 1979. *Homosexuality in Perspective.* Boston: Little, Brown.

Mauss, Marcel. (1935)1973. The Techniques of the Body. *Economic Sociology* 2:75–88.

Mead, George Herbert. 1968. *The Self in Social Interaction.* New York: John Wiley.

Mead, Margaret. 1928. *Coming of Age in Samoa.* New York: William Morrow.

———. 1930 *Growing Up in New Guinea: A Comparative Study of Primitive Education.* New York: William Morrow.

———. (1935)1950 *Sex and Temperament in Three Primitive Societies.* New York: Mentor.

Messenger, John. 1969. *Inis Beag: Isle of Ireland.* New York: Holt and Winston. Reissued Prospect Heights, IL: Waveland Press, 1983.

Michael, Robert T., John H. Gagnon, Edward O. Lauman, and Gina Kolata. 1994. *Sex in America: A Definitive Survey.* Boston: Little, Brown.

Middleton, DeWight R. 1989. Emotional Style: The Cultural Ordering of Emotions. *Ethos* 17:187–201.

———. 1998. *The Challenge of Human Diversity.* Prospect Heights, IL: Waveland Press.

Molnar, Steve. 1983. *Human Variations: Races, Types, and Ethnic Groups*, 2nd edition. Englewood Cliffs, NJ: Prentice Hall.

Monto, Martin A. 2000. Why Men Seek Prostitutes. In *Sex for Sale: Prostitution, Pornography and the Sex Industry*, Ronald Weitzer (ed.), pp. 67–84. New York: Routledge.

Mosher, Celia D. 1980. *The Mosher Survey: Sexual Attitudes of 45 Victorian Women*. New York: Arno.

Murdoch, George M. 1949. *Social Structure*. New York: Macmillan.

Murray, Stephen O. and Will Roscoe. 1998. *Boy-wives and Female Husbands: Studies of African Homosexualities*. New York: St. Martins.

Nanda, Serena. 2000. *Gender Diversity: Crosscultural Variations*. Prospect Heights, IL: Waveland Press.

Nelson, Sara M. 2001. Diversity of the Upper Paleolithic "Venus" Figurines and Archaeological Mythology. In *Gender in Cross-Cultural Perspective*, 3rd ed., Caroline B. Brettell and Carolyn F. Sargent (ed.), pp. 82–88. Upper Saddle River, NJ: Prentice-Hall.

Pasternak, Burton, Carol E. Ember, and Melvin Ember. 1997. *Sex, Gender, and Kinship: A Cross-Cultural Perspective*. Upper Saddle River, NJ: Prentice Hall.

Perper, T. 1985. *Sex Signals: The Biology of Love*. Philadelphia: ISI Press.

Rahman, Anika and Nahid Toubia. 2001. *Female Genital Mutilation: A Practical Guide to Worldwide Laws and Policies*. New York: Zed (Palgrave).

Rathus, Spencer A., Jeffrey S. Nevid, and Lois Fichner-Rathus. 2000. *Human Sexuality in a World of Diversity*. Boston: Allyn and Bacon.

Regis, Helen A. 1995. The Madness of Excess: Love Among the Fulbe of North Cameroun. In *Romantic Passion: A Universal Experience,* William Jankowiak (ed.), pp. 141–51. New York: Columbia University Press.

Relethford, John H. 2000. *The Human Species: An Introduction in Biological Anthropology*, 4th ed. Mountain Valley, CA: Mayfield.

Rich, Grant Jewell, and Kathleen Guidroz. 2000. Smart Girls Who Like Sex: Telephone Sex Workers. In *Sex for Sale: Prostitution, Pornography, and the Sex Industry*, Ronald Weitzer (ed.), pp. 35–48. New York: Routledge.

Roscoe, Will. 1998. *Changing Ones: Third and Fourth Genders in Native North America*. New York: St. Martins.

Rosenblatt, Daniel. 1997. The Antisocial Skin: Structure, Resistance, and "Modern Primitive" Adornment in the United States. *Cultural Anthropology* 12(3): 287–334.

Rubin, Gayle. 1984. Thinking Sex. In *Pleasure and Danger: Exploring Female Sexuality,* Carole Vance (ed.), pp. 207–19. Boston: Routledge.

Sanday, Peggy. 1981. *Female Power and Male Dominance: On the Origins of Sexual Inequality*. New York: Cambridge University Press.

Seabrook, Jeremy. 1996. *Travels in the Skin Trade: Tourism and the Sex Industry*. Chicago: Pluto.

Shostack, Marjorie. 1983. *Nisa: The Life and Words of a !Kung Woman*. New York: Vintage.

Sirles, E. A. and P. J. Frank. 1989. Factors Influencing Mother's Reactions to Intrafamily Sexual Abuse. *Child Abuse & Neglect* 13:131–139.

Siskind, Janet. 1973. *To Hunt in the Morning*. New York: Oxford University Press.

Sobo, Elisa J. 1995. *Choosing Unsafe Sex: AIDS-Risk Denial Among Disadvantaged Women*. Philadelphia: University of Pennsylvania Press.

Spear, Jennifer M. 1999. "They Need Wives": Metissage and the Regulation of Sexuality in French Louisiana, 1699–1730. In *Sex, Love, Race: Crossing Boundaries in North American History,* Martha Hodes (ed.), pp. 35–59. New York: New York University Press.

Spiro, Melford. 1958. *Children of the Kibbutz.* Cambridge, MA: Harvard University Press.

Stoller, Paul. 1997. *Sensuous Scholarship.* Philadelphia: University of Pennsylvania Press.

Strathern, Andrew. 1996. *Body Thoughts.* Ann Arbor: University of Michigan Press.

Suggs, David N. and Andrew W. Miracle, eds. 1999. *Culture, Biology, and Sexuality.* Southern Anthropological Proceedings, No. 32. Athens: University of Georgia Press.

Taylor, Timothy. 1997. *The Prehistory of Sex: Four Million Years of Human Sexual Culture.* New York: Bantam.

Tennov, Dorothy. 1979. *Love and Limerance: The Experience of Being in Love.* New York: Stein and Day.

Thornhill, Randy and Craig T. Palmer. 1999. *A Natural History of Rape: Biological Bases of Sexual Coercion.* Boston: MIT Press.

Trexler, Richard C. 1995. *Sex and Conquest: Gendered Violence, Political Order, and the European Conquest of the Americas.* Ithaca, NY: Cornell University Press.

Tylor, Edward B. 1871. *Primitive Culture.* London: J. Murray.

Van Gennep, Arnold. 1960. *The Rites of Passage.* Chicago: University of Chicago Press.

Vance, Carole. 1984. *Pleasure and Danger: Exploring Female Sexuality.* Boston: Routledge.

Wagner. 1975. *The Invention of Culture.* Englewood Cliffs, NJ: Prentice Hall.

Wallace, Anthony F. C. (1961)1970. *Culture and Personality,* 2nd ed. New York: Random House.

Walley, Christine J. 1997. Searching for "Voices": Feminism, Anthropology and the Global Debate over Female Genital Operations. *Cultural Anthropology* 12(3): 405–38.

Walters, Ronald G. 1974. *Primers for Purity: Sexual Advice to Victorian America.* Englewood Cliffs, NJ: Prentice Hall.

Weiner, Annette. 1976. *Women of Value, Men of Renown: New Perspectives in Trobriand Exchange.* Austin: University of Texas Press.

———. 1987. Introduction. In *The Sexual Life of Savages in the Western-Pacific,* by Bronislaw Malinowski. Boston: Beacon.

———. 1988. *The Trobrianders of Papua New Guinea.* New York: Holt, Rinehart & Winston.

Weitzer, Ronald. 2000. The Politics of Prostitution in America. In *Sex for Sale: Prostitution, Pornography, and the Sex Industry,* Ronald Weitzer (ed.), pp. 159–80. New York: Routledge.

———, ed. 2000. *Sex for Sale: Prostitution, Pornography, and the Sex Industry.* New York: Routledge.

Westermarck, Edward. 1922. *The History of Human Marriage.* London: Macmillan.

WHO.int. 2001. World Health Organization. New York.

Wikan, Unni. 1990. *Managing Turbulent Hearts: A Balinese Formula for Living.* Chicago: University of Chicago Press.

Wolf, Arthur P. 1970. Childhood Association and Sexual Attraction: A Further Test of the Westermarck Hypothesis. *American Anthropologist* 72:503–15.

Wolfe, Linda 1999. Human Sexual Behavior and Evolution. In *Culture, Biology and Sexuality,* David N. Suggs and Andrew W. Miracle (eds.), pp. 76–85. Athens: University of Georgia Press.

Wood, John C. 1999. *When Men Are Women: Manhood Among the Gabra Nomads of East Africa.* Madison: University of Wisconsin Press.

Yelvington, Kevin A. 2001. Flirting in the Factory. In *Gender in Cross-Cultural Perspective,* 3rd ed. Caroline B. Brettell and Carolyn Sargent (eds.), pp. 220–31. Upper Saddle River, NJ: Prentice Hall.

Index

141